Lao Tzu and Taoism

MAX KALTENMARK

Lao Tzu and Taoism

Translated from the French
by Roger Greaves

Stanford University Press
Stanford, California

Originally published under the title
Lao tseu et le taoïsme, © 1965 by Editions du Seuil, Paris.
The present edition contains minor additions
and corrections by the author.

subject: Lao-Tzu
Taoism

Stanford University Press
Stanford, California
© 1969 by the Board of Trustees of the
Leland Stanford Junior University
Printed in the United States of America
Cloth ISBN 0-8047-0688-3
Paper ISBN 0-8047-0689-1
Original edition 1969
Last figure below indicates year of this printing:
93 92 91 90 89 88 87 86 85 84

PREFACE

When Editions du Seuil asked me to write a short book on
Lao Tzu for their *Maîtres spirituels* series, I set out with
the intention of limiting my remarks to the philosophy of
Lao Tzu and his disciples, judging that the space available
to me was only just sufficient for an outline of ancient,
philosophical Taoism. But all the books in this series contain much iconographical matter, and the task of illustrat-
ing the texts of the *Tao Te Ching* or even the *Chuang Tzu*
was virtually impossible. I therefore decided to include a
brief treatment of religious Taoism. This meant that I had
to limit my discussion even more severely, but at the same
time it forced me to deal almost exclusively with essentials
—an advantage, perhaps, for nonspecialist readers, who
might easily have been bored by an excess of technical and
scholarly detail. The present edition in English is for the
most part identical with the French edition (although the
illustrations are not included). It therefore suffers from the
same defects, and benefits from the same advantage, if advantage it be. Hence, apart from the odd exception, there
are no notes to justify the translations. However, a section
outlining the main revealed books has been added to Chapter 5, and the bibliography has been expanded to include
English translations of the Chinese texts discussed.

Taoist studies in Western languages are still in their infancy; in the next few years, however, we can expect to see considerable progress, and it may be hoped that, before too long, it will be possible to give a much more detailed account of this fascinating subject.

Paris   M.K.
December 1968

TRANSLATOR'S NOTE

My transpositions of Professor Kaltenmark's translations from the Chinese and those he has cited from Chavannes, Maspero, and Demiéville were guided by the well-known versions in English: Waley's, Lau's, and Wing-tsit Chan's for the *Lao Tzu*, Giles's and Watson's for the *Chuang Tzu*, and Watson's for Ssu-ma Ch'ien's *Shih Chih*. But interpretations of the Chinese texts differ: on those occasions where my guides took different paths from the one chosen by Professor Kaltenmark, I tried to represent the French phrase as literally as English syntax and vocabulary would allow. Translation at one remove is brave, but translation at two removes is foolhardy: I alone am responsible for any misrepresentation.

On questions of terminology, my *vade mecum* was—with the restriction made above—the popular book by Holmes Welch of Harvard.

R.G.

CONTENTS

Lao Tzu and Taoism

INTRODUCTION

Chinese philosophical thinking emerged and developed during a long period of warfare that wrought profound changes in China's political and social structure. In the fifth century B.C., China was still divided into a large number of feudal states; in 221 B.C., the state of Ch'in won supremacy over its rivals, and its leader became the first emperor of a united China, assuming the title Ch'in Shih Huang Ti. The historians' name for these three centuries (the fifth to the third centuries B.C.) is the "Period of the Warring States"; "Period of the Philosophers" would be equally appropriate, for never was speculative thinking so widely and so freely practiced as in those troubled times. Philosophers gradually turned away from traditional religious and moral thinking, and elaborated a metaphysics that was to remain virtually unmodified for centuries, except for a limited borrowing of ideas from Buddhism.

Early in the fifth century B.C., K'ung Ch'iu (Confucius) founded the first school of wisdom in the small state of Lu, in modern Shantung. This event was of unusual importance, for Confucius's doctrine, as developed by his disciples, was destined to leave a deep impression on the Chinese mind, providing the almost immutable bases of moral and political philosophy for more than two thousand years.

Confucius's life (551–479 B.C.) falls at the end of the period preceding the Period of the Warring States, a time when signs of decadence had already become apparent in the social structure and when both the traditional order and the ideals that justified it were in danger. Confucius considered it his mission to save that order and those ideals. His conception of history and society was Utopian: an orderly society, as he saw it, was a society organized on feudal lines, with tradition and religion keeping some sort of balance between the rival barons. Feudalism in this sense refers to more than just economic or juridical relationships; it refers to a system of relationships pervading society as a whole, in its spiritual as well as its material existence. Moreover, ancient Chinese conceptions of nature and the universe were often little more than projections of social values: the world was seen as a hierarchical system modeled on human society. To be sure, human society necessarily conformed to the celestial order; but since the celestial and earthly orders were interdependent and closely linked by "correspondences" and magico-religious "participations," human behavior in its turn had an influence on nature, and the least disorder in society put the whole universe in jeopardy. We can easily understand the anguish of the "intellectuals" who held these views, the custodians of an ancient tradition, when that tradition began to break up before their eyes. They were incapable of imagining any culture but their own, which they believed had existed since the dawn of civilization. Civilization itself was a harmonious corpus of perfect, immutable institutions laid down by the so-called sage-kings of antiquity, the great founders of dynasties, and in particular the kings of the reigning Chou dynasty.

The Chou dynasty succeeded the dynasty of the Shang

(also called Yin) in the eleventh century B.C. The Shang capital was not far from modern Anyang, in northern Honan; archaeologists working on the site where it stood until 1111 B.C. have unearthed various building foundations, tombs, and miscellaneous objects, including the earliest written documents of China.

Despite these discoveries, we still have very little information about the Shang dynasty and the early Chou monarchs. The Chou domain seems never to have been very large, and by the eighth century B.C. the Chou rulers' power had been greatly reduced. The king, who bore the title Son of Heaven, still had religious prestige, and his traditional role as the barons' suzerain and arbiter was still respected. But little by little, as the great feudal lords grew more ruthless in the pursuit of their ambitions, the old rules of conduct lost their authority. Contact with the barbarians forced the peripheral Chinese states to adopt new principles of organization and to change their forms of government, agriculture, and warfare. Population increases and the invention of iron and the plow also contributed to the overthrow of the established order. Confucius attempted to save the edifice of traditional civilization by providing it with deeper moral foundations. Though his attempt failed, his many disciples spread his teachings throughout China; and they did their job so well that Confucianism gradually came to be recognized as the authentic repository of civilization. Unfortunately, not all the Master's disciples were faithful to his thinking. Whereas he had preached an ethics based on the perfecting of the individual mind, a thoroughgoing self-cultivation that he saw as the prime requisite for good government, his successors too often opted for a formalized ritualism. If we except the obligation to study the Confucian Classics (*ching*), the main duties of every respectable member of Confucian society were to observe the rites and to respect the hierarchies.

Though Confucius's school was the first to be founded, it was quick to acquire rivals, which soon became so numerous that the Chinese now call them the "Hundred Schools." One was the school founded by Mo Ti in the second half of the fifth century B.C.: violently anti-Confucianist, Mo Ti condemned both music (which was highly valued by Confucius) and the rites, and preached a doctrine of universal love, heroism, and justice. Unfortunately, his teachings are marred by a simplistic utilitarianism and a mean-spirited aestheticism. Another, typical of the period, was the Legalist school. Resolutely realistic and bent on innovation, the Legalists sought to ensure effective government by the promulgation of universally valid penal laws, and by a rational (and brutal) organization of the state's economy and military power. Still other schools were the Sophists, the Politicians, the Diplomats, and the Strategists. Most important of all, there was the school of philosophers called Taoists, whose patron is said to be Lao Tzu.

This wealth of philosophical schools did not survive political unification. From the Han dynasty on, the only ones to remain active were Confucianism and Taoism. The first became the official doctrine of the monarchy, combined with elements borrowed from other currents of thought, in particular from Legalism. But if official morality and public life were stamped with the die of Confucianism, the influence of Taoism remained alive, and often predominant, in the spiritual life of individuals.

I

LAO TZU

Together with Confucius, Lao Tzu is probably the most eminent personage in Chinese antiquity, and one of those whose names are most familiar in the West. The book that bears his name, which is also known under the title *Tao Te Ching*, has been translated far more often than any other work of Oriental literature. Although the text is difficult and the translations are often little more than fanciful interpretations, Lao Tzu's popularity has never diminished. For all that, we know next to nothing about him. We know so little that specialists, whether Chinese, Japanese, or Westerners, do not even agree on his historicity, some maintaining that he is a purely legendary figure, others conceding that he really lived but holding divergent views on when he lived and on certain episodes in his biography. In the last analysis, these discussions have only limited significance for our purposes. Those concerning the *Tao Te Ching* are more important. But even these we cannot go into here, where we must limit our discussion to the main questions raised by the author and the book.

LAO TAN IN HISTORY

Around 100 B.C. Ssu-ma Ch'ien was working at the first history of China, the *Shih Chi* (Historical Memoirs). This

major work, one of our main sources of information about
ancient China, contains a biography of Lao Tzu. Unfortunately, it is abundantly clear that even at this early date
Ssu-ma Ch'ien had only uncertain and contradictory information about his subject. He frankly admits that he is
puzzled, and simply presents the hodgepodge of opinions
he has managed to collect with an avowal that, all things
considered, no one can be sure what they add up to.

The account of Lao Tzu's origins with which Ssu-ma
Ch'ien opens his biography is itself subject to caution. "Lao
Tzu was a man from the village of Chü Jen, district of
Lai, county of Hu, in the kingdom of Ch'u. His surname
was Li, his given name Erh, and his public name Tan."
Ssu-ma Ch'ien's indication of Lao Tzu's birthplace corre-
sponds to the modern town of Luyi (City of the Deer) in
the province of Honan, about 40 li from the town of Poh-
sien (formerly Pochow) in Anhwei. There was a sanctuary
here as early as the Han period, and a temple, the T'ai-
ch'ing Kung (the Palace of the Great Purity), still stands on
the spot traditionally held to be the philosopher's birthplace;* an imposing statue of Lao Tzu, almost twelve feet
high, stands there also. Nearby, it is possible to visit what are
said to be the tombs of Lao Tzu and his mother. This may
seem surprising, seeing that the Taoists considered both to
be exceptional beings who could never have died like ordinary mortals. For another thing, none of the sources states
that Lao Tzu died or was buried at his birthplace. These
two tombs, if they are tombs, are definitely not authentic.
Furthermore, the Memoirs declare that Lao Tzu disappeared after heading toward the west, into the land of

---

* At least it was still standing, though in poor condition, at the start of the
Sino-Japanese War.

Ch'in, and that some people claim he died there. Local tradition places his tomb at Hwaili (the Village of Pagoda Trees) in Shensi, a few miles west of Sian.

Lao Tzu's names pose problems that are almost unsolvable. According to the cited passage in the *Shih Chi*, Lao Tzu's real name was Li Erh (surname and given name) or Li Tan (surname and public name). The earlier texts never call the philosopher by either of these forms; he is always Lao Tzu (Master Lao) or Lao Tan. If Ssu-ma Ch'ien calls him Li, it is probably because a Shantung family of that name claimed to be the descendants of Lao Tzu; their genealogy appears at the end of Ssu-ma Ch'ien's biography, though their claim is historically worthless. The surname stuck, however, with one important consequence: it led the emperors of the T'ang dynasty (A.D. 618–907) to consider him their ancestor.

But what, then, was his real surname? We don't know, though Lao seems improbable. This word, meaning old or venerable, seems to have been a name often given to more or less legendary sages. Old age was considered to be the sign of great vitality and wisdom. And Lao Tzu was, almost by definition, a very old man: Ssu-ma Ch'ien records opinions that he reached the age of 160 or even 200 or more. Lao's other two names, Erh (ears) and Tan (long ears), are also connected with the idea of long life and wisdom, sages often being portrayed with long ears.

The historian's account of Lao Tzu's career contains three assertions that would be of great interest if they could be considered authentic: (1) Lao Tan was the court archivist of the kings of Chou; (2) he was visited by Confucius; (3) he finally went off toward the west, dictating his book during the journey, and then disappeared without a trace.

The meeting between Lao Tzu and Confucius is famous; if true, it would allow us to assign an approximate date to Lao Tzu's activities. Here is Ssu-ma Ch'ien's account of it:

When Confucius went to Chou, he asked Lao Tzu to instruct him in the rites. Lao Tzu replied, "Even the bones of those you mention have fallen into dust; their only remains are their words. Furthermore, when a gentleman lives in favorable times, he hastens to court in a carriage; but when he lives in unfavorable times, he drifts with the wind. I have heard it said that a good merchant hides his wealth and gives the appearance of want; if endowed with a rich supply of inward virtue, the superior man has the outward appearance of a fool. Get rid of that arrogance of yours, all those desires, that self-sufficient air, that overweening zeal; all that is of no use to your true person. That is all I can say to you." Confucius withdrew and told his disciples, "I know a bird can fly; I know a fish can swim; I know animals can run. Creatures that run can be caught in nets; those that swim can be caught in wicker traps; those that fly can be hit by arrows. But the dragon is beyond my knowledge; it ascends into heaven on the clouds and the wind. Today I have seen Lao Tzu, and he is like the dragon!"

The meeting is related again in another chapter of the *Shih Chi*, but Lao Tzu's discourse is different:

When he took his leave, Lao Tzu saw him off, saying, "I've heard it said that the man of wealth and power makes parting gifts of money, and that the good man makes parting gifts of words. I could never be a man of wealth and power; but I sometimes dare to think myself a good man. So I will show you out with a few words, which are as follows: The man who is intelligent and clear-sighted will soon die, for his criticisms of others are just; the man who is learned and discerning risks his life, for he exposes others' faults. The man who is a son no longer belongs to himself; the man who is a subject no longer belongs to himself."

As Edouard Chavannes, the translator of the *Historical Memoirs*, points out, this speech is a condemnation of the intelligence, filial piety, and loyalism that are the essential principles of Confucius's teachings.

This scene was so popular in Han times that sculptings of it can be seen on several Shantung tombstones dating from the second century B.C. We continually come across accounts of it in both Taoist and Confucianist writings; unfortunately, the accounts give differing versions of the place, the date, the number of meetings that occurred, and what Lao Tzu said or did not say, with the result that it is hard to believe that the two great philosophers ever met at all.

For a while, then, Lao Tzu took up residence at court, but in time, perceiving the decadence of the House of Chou, he left, heading west toward the state of Ch'in. The way led through the Han-ku Pass, whose keeper, Yin Hsi or Kuan Yin, begged Lao Tzu to compose a book for him. To comply with this request, the philosopher wrote "a book divided into two sections and containing more than five thousand characters, in which he set forth his ideas concerning the Tao and Te; then he departed and nobody knows what became of him." The Keeper of the Pass (Kuan-ling) Yin Hsi, has become an important Taoist personage; he has even been credited with the authorship of a book, the *Kuan Yin Tzu*; however, he is most probably purely legendary.

Ssu-ma Ch'ien later mentions two well-known figures whom some people identified with Lao Tzu: Lao Lai Tzu, a contemporary of Confucius, and the great astrologer and archivist Tan, who lived much later and who made an obscure prediction in 376 B.C. concerning the destiny of the Chou and their elimination by the state of Ch'in. The historian then concludes: "No one in the world can say whether all this is true or not. Lao Tzu was a hidden sage."

Thus Ssu-ma Ch'ien frankly admits to uncertainty: all the material he has managed to gather about Lao Tzu is so vague and contradictory that he cannot draw a single definite conclusion from it. He explains this dearth of information by describing Lao Tzu as a "hidden sage" and summing up his teachings as follows: "Lao Tzu cultivated the Tao and the Te; according to his teachings, men must strive to live in an obscure and anonymous manner." The description of the philosopher as a "hidden sage" suggests that after leaving his post at the royal court Lao Tzu lived in obscurity. Throughout China's history there have been men who, though members of the intellectual class, have chosen to remain aloof from public life, shunning the cares and rewards of the world, which in all candor they considered a morass.

Confucius, who had occasion to meet some of these people, found their ideas distinctly Taoist in character. One of them was Lao Lai Tzu (the same Lao Lai who was sometimes identified with Lao Tan). According to Chuang Tzu, Lao Lai Tzu harshly reproached Confucius for his narrow-mindedness and pride—faults that were frequent enough, no doubt, in certain teachers of moral philosophy, and that the Taoists were fond of attributing to Confucius himself. Another "hidden sage," the Madman of Ch'u, sang at Confucius's door: "O Phoenix, Phoenix, how your virtue has degenerated! Your past I cannot set to rights, but for the future there is still time to save you. Desist! Desist! In these days men who serve the government are in danger!" (*Analects*, xviii, 5).

People of this persuasion often adopted the peasantry's rustic way of life, or, in the regions of rivers and lakes in the state of Ch'u, the ways of simple fishermen. Others, more radically inclined, took refuge in the mountains, beyond reach of civilization and princely influence. The very existence of these extremists, especially the more radical, challenged everything a prince stood for and was, in effect, a permanent condemnation of his reign. But authority had no hold over them: their superior holiness made them inviolable. There was only one way for a prince to get rid of a troublesome sage: to offer him the throne in the hope that this insult would make him jump into the river holding a rock—as several sages actually did, according to Chuang Tzu.

These hermit sages have played an important role in the history of Taoism: indeed, most of the ancient Taoist philosophers lived in just this way, refusing to take part in public life. Among them were Chuang Chou, the author of the *Chuang Tzu*, Lieh Yü-k'ou, the supposed author of the *Lieh Tzu*, and doubtless many others who are unknown to us. Ssu-ma Ch'ien was therefore reasonably correct in putting Lao Tan in this category.

It would be wrong to imagine, however, that all the hermits were Taoists. Indeed, the Taoists took some hermits severely to task for their fanaticism and puritanic zeal, which marks them out as embittered Confucianists rather than as disciples of Lao Tzu. When the Taoists opted for a life of obscurity, they did so on principle and not out of resentment. Sages like Lao Tzu and Chuang Tzu differed from all other hermits in still another way: they had schools of followers. These schools probably existed as small, tightly exclusive groups, in which over many years an essentially oral teaching was transmitted from masters to disciples, the latter sometimes taking notes. This was, in fact, how most of the ancient books were written; only much later on, it seems, did the masters begin directly composing their own works. What, then, were the circumstances surrounding the composition of the *Tao Te Ching?* In the end that is the question that concerns us, for Lao Tzu the man remains shrouded in impenetrable obscurity.

THE TAO TE CHING

The book attributed to Lao Tzu was originally given the title *Lao Tzu*, in keeping with the practice followed for almost all the ancient philosophers. Thus Meng K'o's (Mencius's) work is called the *Meng Tzu*, Hsün Ch'ing's is called the *Hsün Tzu*, and Chuang Chou's is called the *Chuang Tzu*. The title of *Tao Te Ching* (Sacred Book of the Tao and the Te) was accorded the *Lao Tzu* under the Han; the effect was to give it the same status as the Confucian Classics, which had long since been called *ching*. The character *ching*, whose basic meaning is "warp of cloth," here means "moral canon." The *ching* comprise teachings of outstanding moral value; they are sacred texts revealed by Holy Men or gods. The Buddhists later borrowed the term *ching* to translate "sūtra."

The *Tao Te Ching* is also frequently referred to as the *Book of Five Thousand Characters*. In fact, the existing text has more, and the number varies from version to version. The book is split up into 81 short chapters divided into two parts, the first part ending with Chapter 37. The division into two parts, upper and lower, is of ancient date, but the division into chapters varies in the early versions. The number 81 was chosen because of the mystical value of nine and three. The upper part is sometimes referred to as *Tao Ching* (Book of the Tao), and the lower part as *Te Ching* (Book of the Te), but in the existing version the only justification for this distinction is that Chapter 1 deals with the Tao and Chapter 38 with Te.

If Lao Tan, a contemporary of Confucius, is the author, as tradition says he is, the work dates from the sixth century B.C. However, most scholars believe that the *Lao Tzu* cannot have been written at so early a date, and various other dates have been proposed. Western scholars generally plump for the end of the fourth century B.C. or the beginning of the third century, but their arguments are rather vague. Recent work in China and Japan (the Japanese analyses are particularly thorough) has proved the following points beyond all doubt: (1) that the existing text cannot have been written by Lao Tan, the contemporary of Confucius; (2) that a text similar to the one we possess existed at the end of the Warring States period; (3) that many aphorisms found in the *Tao Te Ching* were well known in Chinese philosophical circles from an early date and were not always attributed to Lao Tan.

Scholars have observed, moreover, that neither the style nor the thought of the book is internally consistent. Some passages are in rhyme and others not; in the rhymed passages there are several very different meters. An examination of the rhymes reveals anomalies that can be accounted for only by assuming that they occur in passages written down in different periods or different regions. As for the content, a considerable number of passages are closer to the tenets of such schools as the Legalists, the Politicians, and the Strategists than to Lao Tan's thought as the ancients understood it, which is the dominant strain of the book. These passages are not clumsy interpolations, however, but a result of the way the *Lao Tzu* was compiled.

We should not think of the philosophical schools of ancient China as exclusive sects. Even the two schools that appear to be the most distinctive—those of Confucius and Mo Ti—were far from being closed groups. Above all, no Taoist school as such existed before the Han. It was the Han historians and bibliographers who drew up a classification of the ancient philosophers by schools, one of which they called the school of the Tao (*tao chia*). During the philosophers' own era they were not as a rule classified into distinct movements, and it is accordingly not always easy to label them. Given these circumstances, it is conceivable that different currents of thought may have derived from common sources and authorities, and that philosophers of various schools took pleasure in ascribing apothegms to such universally revered sages as Lao Tan of the Long Ears or the Yellow Emperor, Huang Ti. The Taoists considered Huang Ti, a purely mythical figure, as much their founder as Lao Tan; many works were ascribed to him, and during the Han dynasty Taoism was known as the "Huang-Lao" doctrine. Early quotations from the writings of Huang Ti have survived; some of them are very similar in style to the *Tao Te Ching*, and in one case (Chapter 6) the text is identical.

All things considered, the *Lao Tzu* appears to be an anthology of apothegms borrowed partly from the common stock of wisdom, partly from various proto-Taoist schools. The anthology was built up gradually and did not take on a more or less definitive form until the third century B.C. Before then many different versions must have been in circulation, which explains the extremely numerous variants found in the various recensions of the existing text as well as in the ancient citations. Indeed, it is possible that as far back as the sixth century B.C., a stock of aphorisms in verse served as a basis for oral instruction in the close-knit groups of "Taoists." These groups differed from the other philosophical schools by virtue of their quietist and mystic ideal. It was in them that true philosophical thinking first began to develop. Thus, surprisingly enough, Taoism came to influence Legalism, whose spirit is the opposite of quietism, partly because it alone offered the ontology that Legalist theory needed.

It is certain that the *Tao Te Ching* cannot have been written by Lao Tan in the sixth century B.C., and the attribution to the great astrologer Tan of the fourth century B.C. is without serious foundation. We must face the fact that we simply do not know by whom, where, and when the work as it has come down to us was compiled; we must also realize that it is, to a significant extent, composite. Clearly, however, its ideas are carefully worked out and form a coherent whole. We must, then, posit the existence of a philosopher who, if he did not write the book himself, was the master under whose influence it took shape. There is no reason why we should not go on calling this philosopher Lao Tan or Lao Tzu, and that is what we shall do, if only for the sake of convenience, in our discussion of the *Tao Te Ching*. We should bear in mind, however, that Lao Tzu may in fact be several thinkers, and that the personality of the last man to have had a hand in the text, probably in the first half of the third century B.C., may have played a central role in determining the version that has come down to us.

THE COMMENTARIES

If the *Tao Te Ching* has been frequently translated in the West, in China itself it has probably been glossed more often than any other work. The list of commentaries, from the third century B.C. down to the present day, amounts to well over two hundred titles. The earliest comments are preserved in two chapters of the *Han Fei Tzu*, the most famous of the books produced by the Legalist school. If Han Fei (269–33 B.C.) is really the author, these notes date from the middle of the third century B.C. Though written by a non-Taoist, the commentary, which deals with only part of the *Lao Tzu*, is very interesting, for it shows how the Legalists, whom Ssu-ma Ch'ien associated with the doctrinal traditions of Huang Ti and Lao Tzu, interpreted the *Tao Te Ching*.

Though Taoism enjoyed great favor under the early Han, no commentaries dating from this period have come down to us. The famous commentary supposed to have been composed by Ho Shang Kung (the Sage of the Riverside), which purports to date from the reign of Emperor Wen (180–57 B.C.), definitely belongs to a later period, though exactly when it was written is impossible to determine. For a long time it was regarded as a belated product of the Taoism of the Six Dynasties, but there is now reason to believe that the manuscript should be dated toward the close of the Han, in the second century A.D. All we know about the author comes from a famous legend, which is related in the preface to the commentary as follows:

Emperor Wen was fond of the sayings of Lao Tzu, but there were many passages that he could not understand, and he could not find anyone to explain them to him. So when he learned of the exis-

tence of a venerable Taoist who lived in a thatched hut by the riverside and read the *Tao Te Ching* assiduously, he sent a messenger to
ask him about the hard passages; but Ho Shang Kung insisted that
the Emperor take the trouble to come himself. So Wen Ti went to
see him, but promptly set to scolding the sage for his arrogance:

"There is no place under heaven that is not the domain of the
King. There is no inhabitant of this domain who is not the vassal
of the King. . . . Even though you possess the Tao, you are still one
of my subjects. Are you not overreaching yourself by refusing to bow
down? Bear in mind that I can make any man I please rich or poor,
powerful or wretched."

Ho Shang Kung immediately rose above his seat and hovered in
midair at a great height. Then, addressing the Emperor, he said,
"Being neither in heaven, nor among men, nor on earth, am I still
your subject?" Wen Ti realized that he was dealing with a supernatural figure, apologized, and thereupon received from Ho Shang
Kung the *Tao Te Ching* with his commentary.

Another early commentary of note is due, by contrast, to
a well-known figure, Wang Pi (A.D. 226–49). This exceptionally gifted young man found the time to write several
works, the most famous being his commentaries on the *I
Ching* and the *Lao Tzu*, before dying at the age of 23. He
is the most distinguished representative of the post-Han
revival of philosophical speculation, which had died out in
the first years of that dynasty. The metaphysical character
of his commentary distinguishes it from the more practical
commentary of Ho Shang Kung.

There can be no question here of giving even a brief account of the innumerable commentaries that have been
written over the centuries. Yet they deserve to be studied
in their own right. It is remarkable to find among the commentators representatives of all three great Chinese ways
of thought: Taoists, of course, but also Confucianists and
Buddhists. We also come across the names of several em-

perors (the commentary by Emperor Hsüan Tsung of the T'ang is one of the most respected of all), men of letters, and famous statesmen. This range of commentators shows the important place that the *Lao Tzu* has always held in the intellectual life of China, an importance extending well beyond purely Taoist circles.

II

THE TEACHING

ANCIENT VIEWS OF LAO TZU'S IDEAS

At the close of the Warring States period, Lao Tan enjoyed the status of an old sage, whose sayings people liked to quote; he was accorded this status by philosophers of almost all schools. It was naturally in the works of Taoist authors, and in particular the *Chuang Tzu*, that Lao Tzu figured most frequently. But this anthology of sayings compiled by Chuang Chou and others can add nothing to our knowledge of the hypothetical Lao Tan; for both the real and the imaginary characters that appear in it say practically nothing that is not fictitious. However, the final chapter, written by an unidentified disciple of Chuang Chou, has a particular merit: it gives an objective account of the main currents of thought in ancient China, and is accordingly invaluable as a document.

Other works contain citations of varying degrees of closeness to the existing text of the *Lao Tzu*. Two of them, the *Lü-shih Ch'un-ch'iu** and the *Hsün Tzu*, offer brief, general criticisms of it. Before we look at what the *Chuang Tzu* has to say about Lao Tzu, it seems of interest to quote these

---

* Written by a group of scholars gathered together under the patronage of Lü Pu-wei, minister of Ch'in Shih Huang Ti.

two criticisms. Here is what we find in the *Lü-shih Ch'un-ch'iu*: "Lao Tan set great store on suppleness" (Chapter 17). "The Holy Man hears that which is without sound and sees that which is without form. Lao Tan, among others, was such a man" (Chapter 18).

For his part, Hsün Tzu, the great Confucian philosopher (*fl.* third century B.C.), says: "Lao Tzu understood looking inward, but knew nothing of looking outward." Further on he adds: "If there is merely inward-looking, and never outward-looking, there can be no distinction between what has value and what has not, between what is precious and what is vile, between what is noble and what is vulgar" (Chapter 17). Hence suppleness and inward-looking were Lao Tzu's ideal of conduct; they led him, according to Hsün Tzu, to neglect hierarchical relationships and values, those fundamentals of Confucian society. We must note, however, that Hsün Tzu was writing on the eve of the founding of the Ch'in empire; his ethic was necessarily different from the ethic of the old Confucianism, which by no means condemned a certain amount of accommodating suppleness. Knowing how and when to yield was an art taught by the rites, so it would seem that suppleness and humility were not specifically Taoist virtues. But Lao Tzu's attitudes had nothing at all to do with the rites, and that is why Hsün Tzu, who advocated basing government and education on the rites, condemned his views as dangerous.

The passage from Chapter 18 of the *Lü-shih Ch'un-ch'iu* quoted above suggests that Lao Tzu had the gift of mystical intuition, and he is credited with a similar gift in the paragraph about him in the T'ien-hsia chapter of the *Chuang Tzu*:

To regard the root of things as a pure essence and the creatures around us as coarse stuff, to see multitude as deficiency, to stand serenely and alone in the presence of the sacred powers—this was one of the teachings of antiquity. Kuan Yin and Lao Tan heard of this teaching and accepted it wholeheartedly. They made its basic principle the Permanent Unseen and its ruling idea the Supreme One. Their outward demeanor was gentle and accommodating; their inward principles were perfect emptiness and noninjury to all living creatures. [Chapter 33]

This passage, which reflects the Taoist point of view, once again invokes Lao Tan's humility. But here humility is no longer the sages' essential attitude but something exterior, superficial; their essential attitude is the Void. We shall see that this term means not only absence of knowledge but also absence of desire and will; hence it meant absence of all aggression tending to harm other people. Note that this passage links Kuan Yin and Lao Tzu to an ancient tradition, seemingly of mystic origin, which they are said to have enriched with new metaphysical concepts.

Another summary of Lao Tzu's thought can be found in the *Historical Memoirs* of Ssu-ma Ch'ien. According to this historian, the philosopher's doctrine was centered on the ideas of the Void and the Unseen; he adds the notion of inaction (*wu-wei*), which enables the sage to adapt to worldly change. In his afterword, Ssu-ma Ch'ien cites a passage from his father Ssu-ma Tan. This passage, an account of the various philosophical systems, lays great stress on Taoism, which Ssu-ma Tan ranked above the other doctrines: here again, the main points are inaction, adaptation to change, and the Void.

It may seem surprising that these summaries do not stress the Tao and Te: are these not, after all, the fundamental notions of our philosopher? Surely his doctrine is first and foremost the "Doctrine of the Tao"? In fact, the omission is more apparent than real, for these notions are designated here by other terms, which, as we shall see, connote modalities of the Tao: the Unseen, the Supreme Unity, *wu-wei*, etc. If these terms are preferred to Tao and Te, it is because Tao and Te are not peculiar to Taoism, but belong to the common vocabulary of philosophy and religion, and so could hardly be considered distinguishing characteristics of the thought of Lao Tzu. It is a fact, nonetheless, that in the *Tao Te Ching* they are invested with new value, and this justifies the title given (at a late date) to the book, as it justifies the name of the school.

TRADITIONAL NOTIONS OF TAO AND TE

The root meaning of Tao is "path" or "way." When used as a verb, the same word (with sometimes a slight variation in the script) means "to direct," "to guide," or "to establish communication." A person directs another by telling him the way he has to follow, so Tao also means "to say" or "to tell." And insofar as saying or telling is the same as informing and teaching, Tao has the further meaning "doctrine."

Above all, then, the word Tao suggests a way to be followed and, by extension, moral guidance or a code of behavior. In what are properly called Confucian texts it usually has this extended meaning. But before entering the Confucian vocabulary, Tao had acquired quite different connotations. In the terminology of religion and magic it designated the art of establishing communication between Heaven and Earth, between gods and men, and of performing magical or technological feats. Tao in this sense is at once an art, a method, and a power—the mysterious power of the soothsayer, magician, and king. There was a time in China, as in many other lands, when the rulers were scarcely different from magicians. In historical times, the Chinese kings and emperors kept about them an aura of this wizardry. They were supposed to possess a "virtue," Tao or Tao-te, by which they could impose order, not only on their subjects, but on all of nature as well. To understand more clearly the links between these notions of Way and Order in ancient Chinese religious thinking, we might do well to look at an old myth. One of the most famous of all the heroes of the legendary era is Yü the Great, the founder of the Hsia dynasty (which, until proven otherwise, must be considered purely mythical). Yü was a kind of demiurge who rid China of a great flood; he drained off the waters, which were threatening to rise up to the heavens, by opening up a way (*tao*) for them through the mountains. Then he "visited and put in order [*tao*]" the nine provinces of the world. (The mystical meaning of "nine" is totality.) He civilized the earth and made it fit for men to inhabit by controlling the flow of the rivers and establishing communication among the various parts of the world. Throughout his labors Yü was aided by fantastic creatures drawn by his virtue.

We can see from this how the word Tao could designate the civilizing power of the exemplary sovereigns, and then that of the kings, who periodically had to restore order in nature with the aid of rites. The most important of these rites was undoubtedly a circumambulation: the king toured the empire sunwise, or, at fixed times of the year, moved around the inside of a temple whose structure reproduced that of the universe. In fact, a Son of Heaven's whole life had to be regulated according to the natural order; this is what was called the Royal Order or Way (*wang tao*) in imitation of the Heavenly Order or Way (*t'ien tao*). This heavenly or natural order, often called simply Tao, was held in classical thinking to be primarily observable in the regular alternation of the seasons and of night and day. This cycle of hot and cold, light and darkness, was said to reflect the alternating influence of two sexual principles, the Yin and the Yang, which governed the behavior of all creatures. The Yin, principle of darkness, cold, and femininity, invited withdrawal, rest, passivity; the Yang, principle of light, heat, and masculinity, incited expansion, activity, even aggression.

In traditional philosophical and religious thinking, the Tao is therefore Order, or rather the Principle of Order, which can manifest itself in various domains of the real. Hence the references not only to Heavenly Tao and Royal Tao, but also to Tao of the Earth and Tao of Man. The Tao of the Earth is opposed to the Tao of Heaven in much the same way as the Yin is opposed to the Yang; in this context "Tao of Heaven" takes on a more limited meaning, and no longer stands for Nature as a whole, but for the action of the stars and planets, a purely Yang activity as against the Yin activity of the earth. Accordingly, the alternation of the Yin and the Yang was imagined to be the same as that of the influences of Earth and Heaven. Furthermore, all creatures, and man in particular, are composed of a mixture of celestial and terrestrial elements, and that is why the universe is composed of "three powers": Heaven, Earth, and Man. Man is the religious intermediary between Heaven and Earth, but strictly speaking, only the Son of Heaven can adequately perform this task, for he alone is empowered to sacrifice to the Heaven of his ancestors. The Tao of Man comprises all the principles of behavior that enable man, in the person of the king, to play this role of intermediary; it was this Tao that represented the ideal of Confucius, who proclaimed: "He who hears of the Tao in the morning can die peacefully in the evening." This ideal was approached through study and sincere practice of the Confucian virtues. The Celestial Tao, however, was a subject about which the Master's agnosticism (or perhaps his religious scruples) forbade him to speak. Yet the School of Literati could not do without a metaphysics altogether; Confucius's successors added to the list of Classics, or canonical books (*ching*), used for teaching and studying, a collection of philosophical treatises called the *I Ching* (Book of Changes). This strange and obscure work was originally a manual of divination. Essentially, it consisted of a series of symbols—diagrams formed by the combination of solid lines and broken lines. When these lines are combined in groups of three, we get eight trigrams. According to legend, these eight figures were drawn by Fu Hsi, the first of the three legendary rulers, who was a divine being with the body of a serpent. In the terminology of the *I Ching*, the solid lines are called strong or hard (*kang*) and the broken lines weak or soft (*jo*); in general terminology, it is also said that the strong lines represent the Yang and the weak lines the Yin.

When the trigrams are combined in pairs, one above the other, we get 64 hexagrams. The trigrams and hexagrams symbolize the realities, the former more synthetically, the latter more analytically. The symbolism is particularly rich if the trigrams or hexagrams are laid out in a circle representing space-time: we can see immediately how the Yin and the Yang alternate, and how we pass from one reality, designated by a symbol (*ch'ien*) formed solely of Yang and representing Heaven, to another reality, designated by a symbol (*k'un*) formed of Yin lines and representing the Earth. Between these two extremes, the other diagrams symbolize intermediate realities, beings, situations, or phases, all allotted varying proportions of Yin and Yang. The technique of divination consisted of picking two of the 64 hexagrams at random, one after the other, and observing the changes in the lines that occurred from one to the other; from these changes, conclusions were reached with the aid of the highly obscure text accompanying each hexagram.

The symbols in the *I Ching* undoubtedly stimulated philosophical reflection from a very early date, as is shown by the appendixes that were added to the manual of divination sometime during the Warring States period. The most important of these little treatises is the *Hsi Tz'u*. It contains the earliest scholarly definition of Tao: "A Yin aspect, a Yang aspect—that is the Tao." And in another appendix (*Shuo-kua*), we find the following explication: "The Tao of Heaven is Yin and Yang; the Tao of the Earth is made up of solid [hard] lines and broken [soft] lines; the Tao of Man consists of the cardinal virtues *jen* [humanheartedness] and *i* [righteousness]." Of course, these three spheres, composed of the same elements, are interdependent and act upon one another. Above all, they are subject to the same rhythm. The ancient Chinese could not conceive of a static universe; to them, everything in the world was animate and changing, and these changes were not linear, but cyclic. There is a feeling of peasant lore behind these cosmological conceptions; but they are due more directly to the observations and reflections of the "learned" astronomers (or astrologers) and physicians (or soothsayers), which made possible the systematizing of popular beliefs. This scholarly thinking developed the great categories of Chinese philosophy: Tao, Yin and Yang, the Five Elements. The Five Elements are themselves spatio-temporal categories rather than "materials." They are situated in space-time as follows: Wood–East, Fire–South, Earth–Center, Metal–West, and Water–North.

After this consideration of the Tao, we must now say a few words about traditional notions of Te. Te is usually translated Virtue, and the compound Tao-te designates what we today call moral philosophy. To Confucius, Te was a quality acquired by living nobly in cultured company. As the possessor of Te, the sage exemplifies an ideal of civilization and becomes a model of behavior for all around him: his virtue is thus contagious, efficacious. The notion of Te always implies a notion of efficacy and specificity. Every creature possessing a power of any kind, natural or acquired, is said to have Te. Tao and Te are thus quite close to each other in meaning, but the former is universal indeterminate Order, and the latter is a virtue or potency enabling a man to accomplish particular actions. It is "the ideal efficacy that becomes particular as it becomes real."* Te, then, has varied meanings ranging from magical potency to moral virtue. But the latter is a derived meaning, for originally Te was not necessarily good: a man who has Te of an inauspicious kind brings misfortune down on himself and others. Never-

* Marcel Granet, *La Pensée Chinoise*, (Paris, 1934), p. 303.

theless, Te is generally used in the good sense: it is an inner potency that favorably influences those close to its possessor, a virtue that is beneficent and life-giving. According to the *Hsi Tz'u,* the Te of Heaven and Earth is none other than their power to give rise to universal life.

THE INEFFABILITY OF THE TAO

The word *tao* can have so many different meanings that it invariably imposes difficulties of interpretation in the passages in which it occurs. A case in point is the *Tao Te Ching,* in which the term occurs 76 times, each time with different connotations. Often the word is used in one of its normal meanings: Natural Law (Tao of Heaven), doctrine, ideal of behavior, etc. But at other times it has a new meaning, one that is not found in the old non-Taoist philosophers. On these occasions the Tao is more than a principle of Order, it is a reality behind the origin of the universe; or rather, *tao* is the word that Lao Tzu, lacking a better term, used for that reality: "There is an undifferentiated yet perfect being, born before Heaven and Earth. . . . We may think of it as the Mother of this world, but I do not know its name [*ming*]; I shall call [*tzu*] it Tao; were I forced to give it a name [*ming*], it would be the Immense [*ta*]" (Chapter 25).

Neither *tao* nor any other word in a human language can serve as a name (*ming*) for the Supreme Principle. For *ming* is the personal, intimate name of the individual, the use of which was forbidden to inferiors, and which was therefore taboo, because to know it and (especially) to pronounce it was to gain a hold on the person named. The true name of the Tao must therefore remain unknown; Tao is only a style (*tzu*), a non-taboo given name for public use. It is true that the commoner meaning of *ming* is "word" or "name" without the precise reference mentioned above, but for the ancient Chinese a *ming* was never entirely without prestige value: for everything that has a name has its place in a hierarchical universe. This is why one of the problems that long preoccupied the ancient philosophers, beginning with Confucius himself, was that of the relationship between words and realities. Some pointed to the arbitrary nature of all naming, the sole justification for which is social custom; others showed that names, especially those referring to ranks and statutes, have a coercive value: they tend to lock living beings into categories and set limits on their activities. This was another reason why no name could be suitable for the absolute. When, nonetheless, Lao Tzu declares that, if he were forced to choose a name for the Tao, it would be Great (*ta*), it is clear that he is using *ta* in an absolute sense: the Immense, the Incommensurable. This use of the word is exceptional. Certain later Taoists, commenting on Lao Tzu's text, preferred to correct it slightly, and instead of *ta* write *ta-i* or *t'ai-i*—Great Unity or Supreme Unity—an expression that the Sophist Hui Shih defined as follows: "The infinitely great has nothing exterior to itself; it is called Ta I."

The ineffability of the Tao is affirmed in the very first chapter of the *Tao Te Ching*. This extremely important chapter is unfortunately one of the most awkward in the whole book, for the possibility of punctuating the text in several ways, the character variants, and the uncertain meanings of particular words justify several quite different

translations. The tentative translation adopted here con-
forms to the punctuation followed by the earliest of the
commentators:

   1. A *tao* that can be told of [*tao*] is not the Permanent Tao
[*ch'ang tao*].
   2. A name that can be named is not the Permanent Name
[*ch'ang ming*].
   3. The nameless is the origin of Heaven and Earth.
   4. The named is the Mother of the Ten Thousand Creatures.
   5. Hence, in the permanent state of undesire, we see its mysteries;
   6. In the permanent state of desire, we see its boundaries [or: its
surface].
   7. These two [modes] have the same principle but different
names.
   8. Together, I call them the Obscure [*hsüan*];
   9. The most obscure in this obscurity is the Gate to all Mysteries.

Ssu-ma Ch'ien says that the *Tao Te Ching* is hard to understand because of its "dark profundity." Certain chapters
are indeed so obscure and ambiguous that a definitive interpretation is impossible. It may be that the obscurity and
ambiguity are intentional, and that these texts were read
and glossed in ways that differed according to the disciples'
levels of initiation. Unfortunately, the only Taoist commentaries we possess are of much later date than the text
itself. Nevertheless, it would be wrong to rule them out
altogether, for in addition to the interest they have in their
own right, they are certainly representative of an ancient
tradition.

   For the first sentence of the above text we shall refer to
the commentary of the *Han Fei Tzu*. Though non-Taoist,
it is interesting by virtue of its early date and because, in a
way, it authenticates the view—contested by certain other

commentators—that the word *ch'ang* should be interpreted in its meaning of "permanent":

> By "perceptible quality" [*li*] we mean the differences between square and round, short and long, thick and thin, sturdy and fragile. When these qualities take definite form [in something], this thing can be told of [*tao*]. Every thing that has definite qualities is subject to the alternations of existing and disappearing, life and death, youth and old age. Every thing that is subject to such alternations cannot be said to be permanent. Only a thing that is born with the universe and that exists without wasting away or aging until the dissolution of the universe can be said to be permanent. Now, this permanent thing is not subject to change and has no definite qualities; having no definite qualities and no spatiality, it cannot be told of. The Holy Man, observing its obscure emptiness on the one hand, and considering its universal effects on the other, gives it the makeshift style [*tzu*] Tao, and can hence discourse upon it. This is why it is written: "A tao that can be told of is not the Permanent Tao."

Note that for Han Fei Tzu the permanence of the Tao means that it is coeternal with the universe (strictly speaking, Heaven and Earth); but he does not seem to think that the Principle antedated the universe. To Lao Tzu, as we have seen, the Tao was born before Heaven and Earth. So in this respect there is a significant difference between the Tao of the Taoists and the Tao of the other schools—even that of the Legalists, for all their being influenced by Lao Tzu's metaphysics.

Hence the first two sentences set up an opposition, on the one hand, between the forms of Tao—i.e. teachings, prescripts, etc.—that can be communicated (*tao*) to others, that can be expressed in words, and the Permanent Tao (*ch'ang tao*), i.e. the Supreme Principle that is not subject to the changes of the phenomenal world. On the other hand, the sentences oppose the names that are used for naming—i.e. those that make beings (including spirits and gods) accessible—to the Permanent Name, i.e. the Name that would adequately represent the transcendent eternity of the Tao.

Ho Shang Kung explains that "the [forms of] Tao that can be told of" are the teachings of the Confucian classics, the doctrines of government and morality; and the "names that are used for naming" are the titles and terms referring to wealth, fame, etc., in other words, the social values, which the Taoists held to be arbitrary and artificial. The true Tao, according to Ho Shang Kung, is at once the formless, nameless Principle of the universe, and the Way, the art of living that consists of letting nature alone, of not intervening in the course of events, an art that has its applications as much in the life of the individual (long life, spirituality) as in politics (letting the people live freely and in peace). As for the True Name, Ho Shang Kung gives a very intriguing interpretation that shows how far a name was from being a mere label: the "spontaneous" and permanent name that the Tao has naturally and essentially "is like a small child that cannot yet speak, like an unhatched egg, a pearl gleaming in its oyster, a fine piece of jade in its rock: though inwardly it is bright with light, outwardly it appears dull and unattractive." We must understand this as meaning that the man who lives in union with the true Tao possesses an interior light, which he carefully hides from view, thereby giving the appearance of a fool; an ordinary *tao* would bring him the renown (*ming* has this meaning too) that the true Tao does not bring him; but to make up for that, he possesses a potential strength (true Te) that comes to him from his permanent union with the Supreme Principle. Ho Shang Kung's glosses are good examples of the Taoist mentality, which saw a close link between metaphysical problems and the art of living.

In lines three and four, if our punctuation—the most natural from a syntactical point of view—is correct, two modes of the Principle are opposed: nameless, named; origin, mother. A further opposition is set down between two phases in the development of the universe: Heaven and Earth are opposed to the Ten Thousand Creatures (all the visible creatures, including man). In a different punctuation, followed by some non-Taoist commentators of the Sung dynasty, these two lines should be translated:

3. Unseen [*wu*] is the name I give to the origin of Heaven and Earth;

4. Seen [*yu*] is the name I give to the Mother of the Ten Thousand Creatures.

Similarly, lines five and six, in the punctuation adopted, imply that the states of desire and undesire are antithetical. But what is meant by "it"? The exegetes have no hesitation in plumping for the human soul. Yet the word permanent (*ch'ang*) in this passage suggests that "it" is once more the Tao. What we must understand therefore is that the Tao has two modes of being: in the state of undesire it is at rest and undifferentiated; in the state of desire it gives birth to differentiated, perceptible beings. But this interpretation does not seem possible in early Taoism, in which the Tao cannot be desiring; for this reason a different punctuation of these two sentences seems to be required. As in sentences three and four, the punctuation sets in opposition *wu* and *yu*, two permanent "aspects" of the Tao:

5. Hence, [in its mode of being] Unseen, we will see its mysteries;

6. [In the world of the] Seen, we will see its boundaries.

The opposition of *wu* and *yu* is fundamental in Lao Tzu's metaphysics and is implied even if the first interpretation is adopted, for *wu*, often translated "nonbeing," properly means "not to have" or "there is not"; and *yu*, generally translated by "to be," means "to have." In their philosophical use these two terms refer to the presence or the absence of perceptible qualities in Being. Comparative philosophy could here find matter for reflection concerning the ontological problem, the problem of being and having. For our part we shall note that *wu* cannot mean nothingness, which would imply a creationist conception foreign to Chinese thinking. On the contrary, it is a superior mode of being; it is also the Void, but we shall see that in Lao Tzu's conception the Void harbors within itself all potentialities. Is *wu*, then, identical with the Tao, as is generally assumed by the exegetes? Certainly not, if by Tao we mean the "Permanent Tao" of the first sentence, which is later called *hsüan*, the Obscure. But it could be just the plain Tao, i.e. the Tao of Heaven (of Nature), which would in that case be a "Tao that can be told of." Is this not what Han Fei means in the commentary quoted above? The Holy Man, considering the universal efficacy of the Principle—without, however, forgetting its obscure emptiness—gives it a name in order to be able to discourse on it. But Han Fei apparently considers the *wu* and the Permanent Tao to be one and the same, whereas Lao Tzu (Chapter 1) distinguishes between the two.

The *wu* is therefore one of the expressible modes of the Supreme Tao; the latter is an ineffable essence, but there is nothing to prevent us from giving the name Tao, conventionally, to one of these modes, and from speaking of it. Yet what can be told of especially is its operation, Te, which manifests itself in the perceptible world. It is at this point that we can bring in the notions of desire and undesire, even if the second translation is adopted. Man lives in the world of perceptible objects, and these perceptible objects excite his senses, his imagination, and his will to power; they drive him to act, to expend his vital energies. So strongly do they force themselves on him that he forgets the other aspect of reality, the unseen world. To those who live in the domain of desires and named, categorized objects, the Taoist master recalls the existence of a form of superior being in which there is nothing to desire and nothing to catalog. But here no doubt we should assume that there was a hierarchy or a progression in the adept's spiritual initiation: after learning that all efficacy is in the Unseen, which is the Origin, he is asked, it seems, to grasp the permanence of the Principle; after the genesis he has to experience a transcendent. And that is what is here called, not the *tao*, but *ch'ang tao* (Permanent or Supreme Tao), or better, the Obscure, the Mysterious (*hsüan*), or better still, the "Obscure more profound than obscurity itself," for there is no end to the plumbing of the mystery.

There is, then, a superior reality that transcends the perceptible and imperceptible modalities of being: that reality is truly ineffable, hence cannot be told of or taught. It is surely not by chance that this affirmation stands at the beginning of the *Tao Te Ching*. The author is warning us that the multifarious doctrines and systems of wisdom or government current in the world are contingent forms of Tao, and that our language cannot express anything but relative truths. It is utterly incapable of expressing the absolute, for which not even an adequate name exists. Lao Tzu implies, therefore, that this supreme reality cannot be considered in his book; only mysteries and revelations concerning the seen and unseen world can be mentioned. However, these mysteries and revelations arise from the depths of the unknowable; the unknowable does in fact have a Mystical Gate, and is hence accessible in some way; or rather, it is the absolute that reveals itself, multifariously and by degrees, to human intuition. A man achieves a vision of reality with a penetration proportionate to the level of wisdom or holiness he has attained. Without claiming to lead him to the terminus, the *Tao Te Ching* will help him to progress along the way by offering him formulas, often paradoxical or enigmatic, calculated to stimulate his meditations. For this book is not a philosophical treatise; it contains no demonstrations of any kind. It gives only conclusions, not the steps by which they are reached; it is up to each man to take the steps on his own.

The Tao is sometimes called a "being" (as in Chapter 25, quoted above), but it is a mysterious being; as soon as we attempt to grasp it via the senses it escapes us:

I search with my eyes but see nothing; I call that the Indistinct [*i*].
I listen but hear nothing; I call that the Silent [*hsi*].
I grope but find nothing; I call that the Subtle [*wei*].
None of these three experiences brings an answer; I find only an undifferentiated Unity.
Its upper part has no light; its lower part has no darkness.
Indiscernible, it cannot be named, for it has already returned to the domain of the imperceptible. [Chapter 14]

What we have here, surely, is an indication of one of the phases in the experience of the mystic, who, in order to encounter the absolute, must first experience absence. He must make a radical renunciation of the senses; if he tries to conceptualize the Tao, it vanishes, for it is none other than the primordial unity of chaos, the unity anterior to the formation of the world. This is why it is rich in potentialities, or Te:

> The Tao is a thing imperceptible, indiscernible.
> Imperceptible, indiscernible! It holds within it the Images.
> Imperceptible, indiscernible! It holds within it the Beings.
> Obscure, dark! It holds within it the Fecund Essences.
> These essences are perfectly pure. It holds within it the Spiritual Essences.
> Throughout time its Name has never left it, for from it issued the Fathers. [Chapter 21]

The name that "has never left" the Tao is no doubt "the Permanent Name" of Chapter 1; "the Fathers" are probably the ancestors of the great families; or perhaps, in a more general sense, the ancestors of each species of beings in this world. In Chapter 62, the Tao is the "granary of the Ten Thousand Creatures"; in Chapter 4 it is their ancestor, a being more ancient than the superior gods, the rulers (*ti*) of the heavens. In point of fact, we are perhaps wrong to speak about Lao Tzu's Tao as "it," for as we shall now see, it appears to be an essentially feminine entity.

THE THEME OF THE MOTHER

The Tao is frequently referred to as the Mother, the progenetrix and foster-mother of all creatures. In Chapter 1, the Tao considered in its "named" or perceptible aspect is called the Mother of the Ten Thousand Creatures. Wang Pi explains this name by referring to Chapter 51, where it is said that the Tao causes all creatures to be born and that Te nourishes them and makes them grow. Wang Pi believes that this Te function of the Tao comes into play when the Principle has form and name. But in Chapters 25 and 52 the appellation "Mother of this world" clearly indicates that the Tao is seen as a first cause. In Chapter 20, Lao Tzu (the Taoist holy man) compares himself with the common people; whereas they enjoy the things of this world, he himself lives austerely, contenting himself with "sucking his mother's breast." By this he means that he derives his physical and spiritual energies (the two were synonymous for the ancient Chinese) from the Tao; and we shall see that this "nourishment" yields, if not immortality, at least long life.

Although the Tao causes all creatures to be born, its role is not always presented as directly procreative. The implication in Chapter 1 is that the Supreme Tao (*ch'ang tao*) produces first *wu* and *yu* (the Unseen and the Seen) and then the Ten Thousand Creatures; it is also said that the *hsüan* (Supreme Tao) produces first *wu* (the Tao as *natura naturans*), then *yu* (Heaven and Earth), and then the Ten Thousand Creatures. Chapter 42 presents this cosmogony in the following terms: "Tao gave birth to One; One gave birth to Two; Two gave birth to Three; Three gave birth to the Ten Thousand Creatures." In this summary of the development of the universe from the primordial Tao to the existence of creatures having form, the numbers symbolize sub-principles which are also steps in the evolutionary process. (It is well known how fond the Chinese were of using numbers to represent qualities instead of quantities.) The assertion that the Tao gives birth to the One is at first glance astonishing, for other passages in the *Lao Tzu*—and indeed the whole Taoist tradition—teach that the One, the symbol of unity-totality, represents the Tao itself. For this reason some editors reject the phrase "Tao gave birth to One" as an interpolation, and follow the reading found in the *Huai-nan Tzu*,* which reproduces Lao Tzu's text without this beginning.

The *Huai-nan Tzu* passage can indeed be useful as a gloss on the *Lao Tzu*, but it does not in itself offer sufficient grounds for correcting Chapter 42. It explains that the action of the Tao begins with Unity, but that Unity, being incapable of imparting life, splits into the Yin and the Yang; and that from the union of the Yin and the Yang the Ten Thousand Creatures are born. "This is why it is said that One gave birth to Two, etc." The beginning has perhaps not been suppressed after all, for it seems to be implicitly contained in the explication that precedes the quotation. Clearly the author of the *Huai-nan Tzu* interprets "Tao gave birth to One" as meaning that the expansion of the Tao has its beginning in the state of undifferentiated unity, and that the states or phases Two and Three are merely modes of the principle in action. Two is the Yin and the Yang, but also Heaven and Earth. Three is the harmonious union of the preceding elements, and also the rhythmic measure of that union, for as the *Lao Tzu* says, three waxings and wanings of the moon make up a season. It was clear, however, to the author of the *Huai-nan Tzu*, that the text of the *Lao Tzu*, as we have it, could lead to confusion, and this no doubt explains why he modified it in his Chapter 3, and also in his Chapter 7.

For my part, I am convinced that the existing version is the correct one. It is confirmed by the following passage in the *Chuang Tzu*, Chapter 12: "At the beginning of all

---

* A collection of philosophical essays written at the court of Liu An, Prince of Huai-nan (d. 122 B.C.).

things, there was the Unseen (*wu*); there was nothing perceptible, there was no name. From this issued the One. There was a unity, but it had no form." Chuang Tzu and Lao Tzu are thus imagining something anterior to Chaos (the One): a kind of absolute void that Chuang Tzu calls the *wu* and Lao Tzu the *tao*. This Tao is thus the *ch'ang tao* of Chapter 1, and the One is the equivalent of the "*tao* that can be named."

Interesting as we may find these speculations and theological niceties concerning the Tao's modes of being, we must not lose sight of the central idea: the Tao is a source of life, the various stages in the formation of the universe are stages in the development of life, and from the central principle a current of life spreads by degrees throughout "creation." This is why the Tao is called the Ancestor or the Mother, terms quite without anthropomorphic implications. The Tao can also be symbolized by a female animal: "The Valley Spirit never dies: it is the Mysterious Female. The gate of the Mysterious Female is the origin of Heaven and Earth. Indiscernible, yet forever present, it is never used up by those who use it" (Chapter 6).

This passage, one of the most esoteric in the book, was later used by religious Taoism to justify various practices that were probably unrelated to its original meaning, though it may well, at some early time, have been given various meanings according to the traditions of the different schools of thought. The symbolism is easy enough to decipher, however, even if we cannot be sure about the reality hidden behind the imagery.

It may be that the Valley Spirit (*ku shen*) was a mythological figure similar to the many found in the *Shan Hai Ching* (Book of Mountains and Seas), which gives a valuable account of the legendary geography of ancient China. Thus Chapter 9 of this book mentions a Valley Spirit of the Rising Sun, who is a water god—doubtless the god of the river flowing through the valley. Could Lao Tzu's Valley Spirit also be connected with water? It probably is, for water plays an important role in Taoist symbolism, and on several occasions Lao Tzu uses the valley image—standing at once for emptiness and for the confluence of waters—as a symbol, either of Te or the Tao, or of the Taoist attitude in general, which amounts to the same thing. But the more precise meaning of *ku* is "mountain spring," so the spirit of a *ku* may well have been essentially the spirit of a spring. The expression "Mysterious Female" (*hsüan p'in*) recalls the dark fecundity of the Tao while suggesting the idea of valley or hollow in the mountains; for "male" and "female" (as used of animals) were terms designating— perhaps in the language of geomancy—the hills and hollows of a landscape.

The text of this Chapter 6 is quoted in the first chapter of the *Lieh Tzu* (which attributes it, not to the *Lao Tzu*, but to a "writing of Huang Ti," the Yellow Emperor) in developing the argument that the unique permanent principle of life and change is opposed to the myriad beings subject to its effects. The principle has no progenitor, has no life of its own creating, and never changes, whereas the created beings are subject to the cycle of birth and death. And the author of the *Lieh Tzu* reminds us that the process of life and change is determined by the alternations and overlappings of the Yin and the Yang, and by the rhythm of the seasons. The Tao, even when symbolized by a female animal, is not a Yin being—which would necessarily have a Yang counterpart—but a solitary (*tu*) entity, single and

autonomous. In addition, this female animal is described as
hsüan, "mysterious"; it is the spirit (*shen*) of the Void, as
symbolized by the valley. *Shen* is defined in the *I Ching*
as anything that has no definite nature, either Yin or Yang;
in this sense every being described as *shen* (divine, spiritual) participates in the undifferentiated nature of the Tao.
Further, like a valley or a spring (*ku*), the word *shen* suggests an idea of fecundity, for it comes from a root meaning
"to pull, to stretch." People believed that women in childbirth were helped by the spirits of the ancestors pulling at
the baby, and no doubt the ancestors were thought to aid
in the same way with the emergence of plants from the
earth. What is more, *shen* is related to another group of
words designating lightning and thunder, both of which
were thought to stimulate fecundity in general and childbirth in particular.

All things considered, Chapter 6 is not so obscure as it
seems at first sight: it suggests that the Tao is a maternal
force, a womb from which the visible world has issued. Sig-
nificantly enough, the *Huai-nan Tzu* quotes Chapter 42 of
the *Lao Tzu* ("Tao gave birth to One, etc.") to introduce a
description of the ten lunar months of pregnancy, suggesting that the development of the fetus and the formation of
the universe are identical processes, though governed by
different rhythms or "numbers." Here we are in the presence of a fundamental Taoist idea: the real, one and mul-
tiple, is no other than a life principle, which is sometimes
concentrated in a single point and sometimes dispersed
among the infinite variety of beings, where it divides into
a variety of particular life functions. Understandably, the
category of sex was quite important in such a conception of
the universe. But in Lao Tzu and the other ancient authors,

the notion of sex remains purely philosophical and symbolic; there is no reason to believe that sexual techniques played a particular role among these mystics, as they did in the practice of certain later Taoist sects.

In Lao Tzu, the idea of mother, female, mystical womb is closely associated with that of emptiness. The Void, which remains one of the great themes of Taoist thought, is referred to poetically and symbolically in Chapters 5 and 11:

The space between Heaven and Earth is like a bellows.
It is empty, but gives a supply that never fails; when it is in motion, it never stops producing. [Chapter 5]

The thirty spokes of a wheel share one hub; but it is where there is nothing [in the hole for the axle] that the efficacy of the cart lies.
We shape clay into the form of a vessel; but it is where there is nothing that the efficacy of the vessel lies.
We pierce doors and windows to make a house; and it is where there is nothing that the efficacy of the house lies.
Thus we think we benefit from perceptible things [the visible and the palpable—*yu*], but it is where we perceive nothing [in the Void—*wu*] that true efficacy lies. [Chapter 11]

The Void is thus none other than *wu*, the absence of perceptible qualities that characterizes the Tao. This Void is efficacious because, like the bellows, it is capable of producing breath at will: the idea expressed is like the one associated with the symbol of the valley. The Void is efficacious for another reason also: like a wheel hub, a vessel, or a house, it is a receptacle. The image of the thirty spokes converging toward the empty space of the hub is often used to symbolize the virtue of the ruler who attracts all creatures to his service, the virtue of Sovereign Unity that brings order to the multiplicity of things around it; but the image can also refer to the being of the Taoist who, when "empty," purified of all passion and desire, is fully inhabited by the Tao or, as Ho Shang Kung puts it, by the vital spirits that animate the body:

In the void between Heaven and Earth, the Harmonious Breath [an equal mixture of Yin and Yang] circulates freely, and the Ten Thousand Creatures are born of themselves. Thus, when man is able to rid himself of his passions, to give up pleasure, and to purify his viscera, then the *shen ming* [spirits and souls from Heaven and Earth] can dwell peacefully within him.

[Commentary on Chapter 5]

RETURNING

All creatures issue from the Tao; they are its children (Chapter 52). But, ineluctably, they must return to its womb. This further idea, central to the thought of the *Tao Te Ching*, is expressed particularly in Chapter 16:

Having attained perfect emptiness, holding fast to stillness, I can watch the return of the Ten Thousand Creatures, which all rise together.

These teeming creatures all return to their separate roots. Having returned to its root, each is still; in stillness, each has returned to its original state. Returning to one's original state is the universal law. To know the universal law is to be illumined; not to know it is to fret in vain and bring down misfortune on oneself.

Knowledge of the universal law is understanding. Understanding leads to impartial universality; impartial universality is perfection. He who is perfect is like Heaven. Being like Heaven, he can identify himself with the Tao. Being identified with the Tao, he can endure, and to the end of his days will fear no danger.

Just as leaves fall to the root of the tree, become humus, then sap, and reenter the cycle of life, living creatures emerge into the perceptible world, then return to the realm of the unseen. From the start, however, the Holy Man stands aloof from this cyclic process: perfectly empty, perfectly calm, he is the possessor of a spiritual light that makes him altogether different from other beings; lacking all particularism, he is indifferent to the realities of this world, but identifies himself with Heaven and the Tao. It is then possible for him to live, if not eternally, at least fearlessly.

The law that everything must return to its starting point is universal because it belongs even to the Tao-as-Nature: "Returning is the movement of the Tao; in weakness lies the efficacy of the Tao. All the creatures in this world are born from the Seen (*yu*); the Seen is born from the Unseen (*wu*)" (Chapter 40).

Essentially, then, in one of its modes, the Tao is movement. If it were not for this movement such things as creatures and life could not exist: there could be nothing but an undifferentiated Unity. Through this movement, which is change, undifferentiated Unity can become multiplicity and still retain its fundamental unity, the principle of all efficacy, of all life (Chapter 39). Thus the movement of the Tao, i.e. its operation, is described as a kind of cyclic movement that recalls the ancient ritual circumambulations we have already referred to: "There is an undifferentiated yet perfect being, born before Heaven and Earth. . . . It revolves throughout the universe and is never halted. We may think of it as the Mother of this world. . . . Were I forced to give it a name, it would be the Immense. Immense, it moves away; it reaches its apogee; it comes back" (Chapter 25).

In the *I Ching*, the hexagram *fu*, signifying the Return (one Yang line beneath five Yin lines) is the symbol of the rebirth of the Yang. At the winter solstice, the Yang seems to have disappeared, whereas the Yin is at its full; but this is the moment when the Yang is reborn and begins its return. Symmetrically, at the summer solstice the Yang is at the apogee of its power while the Yin prepares to return. The alternation of the Yin and the Yang is a going away and a coming back.

The phenomenon of the life and death of creatures is conceived of in the same way: it, too, is an alternation of Yin and Yang, as natural and as ineluctable as the succession of day and night. The Yang stimulates creatures' vitality, but the Yin brings them back to a state of rest, the peace of the Unseen. Only this Tao is not, of course, the Supreme Tao; what is so described is the Tao-as-Nature, or rather, its immanent action (Te).

Conforming to the rhythm of the universe is the prerequisite of wisdom in all Chinese thinking. But the Taoist mystic has greater ambitions than his ordinary compatriots: the question for him is not merely of adapting his ritual and hygienic observances to the alternation of the seasons; he intends to escape from the determinism of life and death by transcending it. This is what enables him to attain inner emptiness: he does not merely witness the return of all creatures to their origin, he precedes them to that origin. "The Mysterious Virtue is profound and far-reaching. [He who possesses it] returns with all things [to the Origin]; and then he attains the Great Harmony [with the Supreme Tao]" (Chapter 65).

Perfect Virtue (*te*) is described as obscure (*hsüan*), like the Supreme Principle itself; the man who possesses Perfect Virtue participates in the life-giving efficacy of the Tao. Lao Tzu calls him by the name *sheng jen*, Holy Man.

THE HOLY MAN

All life is governed by the same permanent law: the return to the origin. To know this law is to possess a superior intelligence that Lao Tzu calls Light (*ming*). But the Holy Man is not content with merely knowing this law intellectually; he realizes it within himself by returning to the Tao in person. The import of this returning is spiritual: it is a matter of identifying oneself with the Tao through an inward realization of its unity, simplicity, and emptiness.

THE CRITIQUE OF KNOWLEDGE AND MORALS

Knowledge of the Tao is no ordinary knowledge. The Taoists condemn mere learning as dangerous, for it is a source of dissipation: its multiplicity destroys the unity of being. In order to maintain or restore unity, and to struggle against the temptations of discursive knowledge, the intellect has to be purified. The first step in this purification is a disciplining of the organs of the senses and passions, for "The five colors blind man's eyes. The five notes deafen his ears. The five tastes deaden his palate. Riding and hunting madden his mind. Hard-to-get goods impede his labors" (*Tao Te Ching*, Chapter 12).

So the Taoist is required to practice a measure of asceticism: the senses are not condemned altogether, but moderation must be observed in their normal use. In Chinese physiology, the sense organs are also "openings," through which vital fluid will escape unless a close watch is kept. The passions cause a gradual loss of life that is, at the same time, a loss of soul. For as Ho Shang Kung points out in his commentary on the above passage, we then lose both our spiritual light and our faculty for hearing the voices of silence, and we can no longer taste the "savor of the Tao."

Contrary to the Confucianists, who make study a basis of their system of morals, Lao Tzu condemns all learning, particularly the pseudoscience of the values taught by the moralists and realists. These philosophers treat values that are as relative as the notions "long" and "short" as if they were absolute. Furthermore, every affirmation of this kind gives rise to the opposite affirmation:

> In this world, everyone recognizes the beautiful as being beautiful, and that is why ugliness exists; and everyone recognizes the good as being good, and that is why bad exists. "There is" and "there is not" produce each other; "easy" and "difficult" give rise to each other; "long" and "short" exist only comparatively with each other; "high" and "low" are interdependent; there are no notes without harmony; there is no "before" without an "after" to follow it.
>
> Therefore the Holy Man ensconces himself in inaction [*wu-wei*], and practices a teaching without words. [Chapter 2]

This relativist attitude is not skepticism, and we shall see that the *wu-wei* is not purely negative. The Taoists considered all social values to be prejudices, and as such, wrong, because they cloud reality and land us in the vicious circle of contradictions. The point is to get out of this circle by transcending it. To do this, we need only look at things from the standpoint of the Tao, for in the Tao all contradictions are reconciled and cancel out. As Lao Tzu says, the Principle is the common refuge of all things and all notions: "The Tao is the mysterious granary of the Ten Thousand Creatures. It is the sacred treasure of the good man, the refuge of the bad" (Chapter 62).

All creatures issue from the Tao and return to the Tao; hence it is their common repository or "granary." Here the text has the word *ao*, which meant the southwest corner of the house, a dark place for storing grain and also the place where the mistress of the house slept. Closely linked with the life and fecundity of the family, it was particularly holy in peasant homes. What the *ao* was to the common people, the treasury (*pao*) was to the nobility: every noble family had a treasury of sacred objects with a protective value, veritable talismans ensuring the happiness and continuity of the family. The Tao, then, is all this: a source of life, of happiness, and of salvation, even for the wicked. The Tao (and the Taoists) reject no one, for in Taoist thinking no one is really good or really wicked: "The Holy Man is a good savior of men and rejects no man; he is a good savior of creatures and rejects no creature" (Chapter 27).

For the evildoer, Virtue is a pole of attraction and a refuge; it converts him to better ways without his knowing it. This is far from being the attitude of the other philosophers, who dogmatically reject everything that contradicts their beliefs. Hence the virtues preached by the Confucianists, for example, are utter degradations of the Tao:

When the great Tao falls into disuse, the virtues of human-heartedness and righteousness arise.
When intellect emerges, the great artifices begin.
When discord is rife in families, dutiful sons appear.
When the State falls into anarchy, loyal subjects appear.

[Chapter 18]

Banish wisdom, discard knowledge, and the people will benefit a hundredfold.

Banish humanheartedness, discard righteousness, and the people will return to the true familial virtues.

Banish ingenuity, discard profit, and there will be no more thieves and brigands.

Something is missing from this threefold advice, so I shall propose this addition: Be without false adornments; preserve inborn simplicity; lessen selfishness and desire; banish knowledge in order to live a carefree life. [Chapter 19]

Humanheartedness (*jen*) and righteousness (*i*) are the supreme virtues of Confucianism. In Mencius they became the foundations of the ethical code of the nobility—the conservative nobility at any rate. Active beneficence, righteousness (i.e. respect for convention, law, and duty), intelligence (where the moral and ritual laws are concerned), filial piety (including the duties inherent in ancestor worship), loyalty (to the ruler)—all these attitudes and notions would be pointless if men knew how to make their behavior conform to the natural order. Every step away from the Tao leads them further and further down the slope toward moral and political anarchy:

The man of superior virtue is not virtuous, and that is why he has virtue.

The man of inferior virtue never strays from virtue, and that is why he has no virtue.

The man of superior virtue never acts, and yet there is nothing he leaves undone.

The man of inferior virtue wants to act, but he is apt to leave things undone.

The man of superior humanheartedness wants to act, but finds no particular occasion for acting.

The man of superior righteousness wants to act, and finds reasons for acting.

The man of the rites wants to act, but meeting with no response, rolls up his sleeves and resorts to persuasion by force.

When people abandon the Tao, they resort to Te; when they abandon Te, they resort to humanheartedness; when they abandon humanheartedness, they resort to righteousness; when they abandon justice, they resort to the rites. The rites are a mere husk of loyalty and faith and the beginning of anarchy. Foreknowledge is merely the glitter of the Tao, and the beginning of folly. Hence a man worthy of this name chooses the solid and not the flimsy, the gem and not the glitter. [Chapter 38]

Lao Tzu is here playing on two different values of the word Te: superior Te is in fact hard to distinguish from the Tao, whose efficacious virtue it is. So the Holy Man has no virtue other than superior Te; he has no virtue, hence merit, particular to himself. On the contrary, the man of "inferior virtue," as Wang Pi explains, takes pride in the virtues, those Confucian virtues that the vulgar people take for goodness. But we know that the notion of goodness implies and gives rise to that of badness: by "never failing in virtue" a man thus moves away from the Tao. Now, if the Tao is absolute perfection, primordial nondifferentiation, even superior Te is already slightly less perfect than it, for it is the start of a descent into the virtues, i.e. into multiplicity. The highest of these virtues, *jen*, or humanheartedness, which in its superior quality is close to inferior Te, is already an activity, but it is still a directionless activity with no reason to manifest itself, i.e. it is not directed at particular objects. But when *jen* becomes a conscious activity limited to particular objects, it is degraded in its turn: a still more inferior virtue crops up, deliberate generosity, righteousness, and lower still, ritual-mindedness, when acts are prompted merely by a desire to make a handsome gesture, by decorum and etiquette. The rites are indeed the opposite of the Taoist ideal; they were instituted to mark distinctions, divisions, and classes. In the relationships that humans have among themselves and with the world, the rites concretize the artificially hierarchized values that official doctrine presents as holy and intangible.

This is why the prime requisite is to repudiate all false wisdom and the pseudosciences, which are nothing more than knowledge of others—and hence pretensions of dominating them; rather, true holiness consists of knowing oneself (Chapter 33). The Taoist can then "know the whole world without crossing the doorstep; see the Heavenly Tao without looking out the window. The further you go, the less you know. Therefore the Holy Man knows without stirring, identifies without seeing, accomplishes without acting" (Chapter 47).

Since the Taoist repudiates pseudoscience for himself, he is naturally against its being taught to others. In Chapter 3, Lao Tzu affirms that the Holy Man rules by "emptying their hearts [their minds] and filling their bellies, weakening their will and toughening their bones, striving to keep the people ignorant and desireless." The formula is undeniably rather harsh, but this is due to the quietists' aversion to the proliferation of all kinds of doctrines that divided the people's minds and led to strife. The "people," in this context, can hardly mean the peasantry; it more likely means the nobility and the philosophers, for they, and not the commoners, are responsible for the proliferation of ideas and ambitions. "Filling their bellies . . . toughening their bones" is to be understood, not as a social economy program, but as an allusion to practices for prolonging life. The expression "filling their bellies" is in no way pejorative in Chinese. Being richly fed was a mark of the aristocracy, and the Chinese have always looked upon stoutness with respect. As for the bones, ancient beliefs held them to be the repositories of the subtlest and most precious life principles. Thus Ho Shang Kung reminds us that chastity results in our having plenty of marrow within solid bones.

Chapter 3, then, does nothing more than proclaim the necessity of renouncing the dangerous temptations of overpolite society in order to return to healthy original simplicity: the heart, the centrifugal seat of the intelligence, the will, and the desires, is opposed to the belly, the centripetal receptacle of the organs of nutrition and the life principles.

WU-WEI

We have several times already come across the expression *wu-wei*: "without doing," "absence of action." *Wu* is not the same as nothingness, and *wu-wei* is not an ideal of absolute inaction; on the contrary, it is a particularly efficacious attitude since it makes all doing possible. "The man who applies himself to study, each day increases [his efforts and ambitions]. The man who applies himself to the Tao, each day diminishes [his activity and desires]. From diminution to diminution, he manages to stop acting altogether; once he has stopped acting, there is nothing he does not do" (Chapter 48). In "ensconcing himself in *wu-wei*," the Taoist merely imitates the Tao, whose efficacy is universal for the very reason that it is "inactive." "The Tao never acts, yet there is nothing it does not do" (Chapter 37).

There is nothing the Tao does not do because the Tao is the same thing as universal spontaneity. Everything in nature comes about of itself, without any particular kind of intervention, such as might be the act of a divinity or of providence. Similarly, the Holy Man takes good care not to intervene: he lets all creatures develop according to their own nature, and thus obtains the best practical results. It is important that the ruler act the part of a Taoist; it is he, in fact, that Lao Tzu has in mind as his reader. The majority of the aphorisms in the *Tao Te Ching* are formulas for good government. Chapter 37 continues:

If lords and kings could be like the Tao and persist in this attitude of nonintervention, the Ten Thousand Creatures would soon follow its example of their own accord; and if they should then show any passion, I would tame them with the simplicity of the nameless, and then they would be passionless. Being passionless, they would be still, and peace would follow naturally.

So the ruler must pass unnoticed:

The best [of all rulers] is he whose existence is unknown; next best is he who is loved and praised; next, he who is feared; next still, he who is despised.

Whoever claims the right to rule over the people must submit to the people in his words; whoever claims the right to guide them must follow them.

Thus the Holy Man dominates without making the people bend beneath his weight; he guides without making the people suffer any harm. [Chapter 17]

Wu-wei is the only means to true success: sooner or later, deliberate intervention always results in failure. "I foresee the defeat of those who would presume to gain power by action" (Chapter 29). And Lao Tzu speaks a warning to men of ambition: the empire that they would conquer is like a precious vessel, easily broken by handling; and "ruling a large kingdom is like cooking small fish," the less stirring up the better (Chapter 60). Not surprisingly, Lao

Tzu points out that it is the law that makes the thief (Chapter 57).

The Holy Man's policy of nonintervention is nothing more than congruity with natural law, the "Heavenly Tao that conquers without striving" (Chapter 73). For Lao Tzu wants to persuade the ruler that *wu-wei* and nonviolence are the most effective means of getting power and holding on to it. Since all action gives rise to reaction, the normal counterpart of a seemingly right action will be wrong. The only action that does not entail this consequence is the natural action of the Heavenly Tao:

> The Tao of Heaven takes away from what has too much, and adds to what has not enough. The Tao of the ordinary man is something else; this Tao takes away from what has not enough and gives it to what has too much already. Who is capable of offering the world what he has in excess? Only he who possesses the Tao.
>
> [Chapter 77]

So *wu-wei* is not pure passivity; indeed, the above passage—which expresses an ideal of social justice quite exceptional in ancient Chinese thinking—goes on to say: "Therefore the Holy Man, when acting, expects no reward for his actions; once the good deed has been done, he does not bask in his merit; he does not show off his talents."

Nothing is more dangerous than vanity, which is so dangerous that the best means of causing somebody's downfall is to lift him up with pride (Chapter 36).

Soldiers too must profit by these principles:

> The good leader in war is not warlike; the good fighter is not impetuous.
> The best conqueror of the enemy is he who never takes the offensive.
> The man who gets the most out of men is the one who treats them with humility.

This is what I call the virtue of nonviolence; it is the strength of the man who knows how to use men.

This is what I call equaling Heaven. Equaling Heaven was the ancients' highest ideal. [Chapter 68]

Oddly enough, the use of arms, though condemned, is not condemned altogether: the Holy Man uses arms solely in self-defense, but he does use them, which is hard to square with what we generally imagine quietist behavior to be like. But we should remember that the *Tao Te Ching* is composite, and that, destined for the ruler as it was, it could not push the ideal of *wu-wei* too far. At any rate, the army leader must be moderate:

He who leads men with the aid of the Tao* takes good care not to wreak violence on the world by use of arms; this kind of action is likely to rebound.

Where armies have passed, only thorns and thistles grow; after great wars there are always years of famine. The good leader in war stops as soon as he has achieved his aim—victory. He does not take advantage of victory to show his strength.

If he is victorious, he is not proud, nor glorying, nor bragging; he gains the victory because he cannot do otherwise; this is why he does so without showing his strength. [Chapter 30]

Arms are ill-omened instruments, and are not the instruments of the Sage; he uses them only when he cannot do otherwise.
[Chapter 31]

Though war is sometimes a regrettable necessity, the leader must use *wu-wei* as a technique to give him an unsung victory. The same holds for the general polity, which must apply the rule of least intervention; but some measure of intervention is doubtless necessary, if only to prevent the intervention of the men of action, the men of in-

---

* Translation in accordance with variant figuring in the texts engraved on stone during the T'ang. The usual text would need to be translated: "He who assists the ruler with the aid of Tao."

telligence (who stir up quarrels), and the merchants, whose commercial interests require them to be forever out after "hard-to-get goods":

It is by not exalting men of talent that rivalries among the people are avoided, by not prizing rare possessions that thefts are avoided. By not displaying things that excite desire, we avoid disturbing the people's minds. Therefore the Holy Man rules by emptying their hearts and filling their bellies, weakening their wills and strengthening their bones, ever striving to make the people knowledgeless and desireless. And he sees to it that those who know dare not interfere. He practices inaction, and all things are brought duly into order. [Chapter 3]

The cases for intervening are therefore the exceptions that prove the rule: the Holy Man always refuses contention; thus no one is ever in a position to contend with him (Chapters 22 and 66).

The attitude of *wu-wei* is undeniably hard to live up to, but it confers true strength on the man who sticks by it, for as Lao Tzu says in a typical paradox, "the soft and the weak overcome the hard and the strong," because weakness, or nonresistance, is the method of the Tao (Chapters 36 and 40). Various symbols serve to illustrate this idea: water, the valley, and the infant:

Greatest perfection is like water, which is the best benefactor of the Ten Thousand Creatures, but which never contends, for it settles in the low-lying places detested by men; and that is why it is so close to the Tao. . . . Because it never contends, it never goes amiss. [Chapter 8]

Nothing in this world is softer or more yielding than water, yet nothing can surpass it for overcoming the hard and the strong. [Chapter 78]

Elsewhere, the low-lying places are themselves the image of the Tao, because the waters converge in them: "If the rivers and seas can be the kings of the valleys, it is because they excel in taking the lower position" (Chapter 66). Indeed, the word king (*wang*) was explained in terms of another word with the same pronunciation meaning "to go toward": the king is the man toward whom people go. His virtue, Te, has the power to attract, and he is essentially an assembler of men and things. The Taoist Holy Man has this royal power; he attracts all creatures toward himself and rejects none. "This is what I call his Veiled Light," says Lao Tzu (Chapter 27). For this Te, this influence that he exerts upon all around him, must, as we have seen, stay hidden and even unconscious. It saves all men and all creatures by bringing them back to their original nature. Hence, "perfect men are the masters of imperfect men; imperfect men are the stock-in-trade of perfect men" (Chapter 27).

Since nobody can become a Taoist by studying, the master referred to here acts solely according to his Te and the example it gives him. Te is his reply to all hostility (Chapter 63), contrary to the wishes of Confucius, who (interpreting Te as "doing good") thought that returning good to all, without discriminating between those who do good to you and those who do evil, was unfair: "Return justice for evil, and good for good" (*Analects*, xiv, 36). But Lao Tzu's words are merely an application of his principle of *wu-wei* and nonresistance.

PRIMACY OF THE FEMININE

The Holy Man's power of attraction comes, then, from his being like a valley, humble and empty: this is the feminine passivity that he has to keep alive at the core of his virile being:

Know masculinity, but prefer femininity: you will be the ravine of the world.

Be the ravine of the world, and Supreme Te will never fail you; and you will be able to return to the state of infancy.

Know whiteness, but prefer blackness: you will be the model of the world.

Be the model of the world and Supreme Te will not fail you; you will be able to return to the absolute of the Unseen.

Know fame, yet prefer ignominy: you will be the valley of the world.

Be the valley of the world, and from Supreme Te you will get your content and be able to return to the simplicity of the uncarved block.

Once the uncarved block is carved, it forms utensils: if the Holy Man used it in this way, he would be fit to be lord over the functionaries. This is why the great craftsman does not carve.

[Chapter 28]

Keep alive within yourself the simplicity and unity of the Tao. Like the Tao, be like a valley; know that, like the Tao, you are male and female, Yang and Yin (i.e. know that you are universal), but opt for the feminine in this double potentiality, for in spite of appearances, the feminine is the more useful of the two. This advice must have seemed presumptuously paradoxical to Lao Tzu's contemporaries. His exaltation of femininity went dead against all conventional thinking. In the hierarchy of the feudal values, the masculine values were the more honorable; the feminine were held to be inferior. This had not always been the case: myth and folklore reveal that women's role in society was once as important, if not more so, than men's, and one aspect of this equality has lingered on in classical religion: the collaboration of the cult leader's wife in the ritual of ancestor worship. Further, the notions of the couple and the sacred marriage held a very important place in ancient Chinese religious thinking. Every sacred power was twofold, male and female; but since only one half of the sacred couple was generally enclosed in any one sanctuary, the ritual was directed at reconstituting the whole. And frequently the better half to have in a sanctuary was the feminine half; for the female attracts the male.

The same broad outline can be seen behind certain shamanistic rituals: dancing priestesses lured male divinities down to possess them. It seems beyond doubt that Lao Tzu's advocacy of femininity was more or less consciously influenced by these ancient beliefs. He has conceptualized them of course, but the basic idea is the same: the complete being is male and female; since most men neglect or repress their feminine nature, they are out of balance; their male aggressiveness comes to the fore, and their whole vitality suffers. There can be no true Holiness without a prior revitalization of femininity.

Once we have appreciated this, we can see why the Holy Man's *wu-wei* is such a superior method of government: it consists of leaving all men, creatures, and things to order themselves spontaneously in accordance with natural harmony, and of not perturbing the order of the Tao through intervening artificially. But the Holy Man's role, though passive, is not negative. He is a pole in this world, a center both of radiation and of convergence: insofar as he has managed to identify himself with the Tao, and insofar as the Tao is femininity or maternal force, he is, like the Tao, both life and a life source. Hence the importance in Lao Tzu, and in the whole of Taoism, of the notion "life principle." The life principle must be carefully maintained, nourished, and concentrated; for, in the last analysis, it is this, the life principle, that is the Tao present in the Holy Man, and that gives him his efficacy, his Te.

LONG LIFE

The quest for long life, indeed physical immortality, has been a characteristic of religious Taoism since the Han period. Various techniques were used to nourish the life energies and expel the death principles. Were these techniques —or at the least some of them—already known and employed earlier in proto-Taoist circles? There is no doubt about the answer, for the philosophers clearly refer to practices for prolonging life; for them, holiness and longevity were closely related.

It is certain that the author of the *Tao Te Ching* considered holiness inseparable from a powerful vitality, which must, of course, remain virtual and concentrated. Excessive activity causes loss of energy: "The Holy Man banishes that which is excessive, that which is swollen, that which is extreme" (Chapter 29). "He avoids being replete" and, thanks to his emptiness, he is assured of seeing his strength renewed in proportion as it is consumed (Chapter 15).

Like heaven and earth, he has no life but the Tao's, which is inexhaustible, as we have seen.

If Heaven and Earth are enduring, it is because they have no life intrinsic to themselves, and that is why they are able to live a long time. Therefore the Holy Man, by keeping to the rear, is always at the fore; by expelling his self, he remains present. Is this not because he is disinterested? This is why he is able to accomplish what serves his interests. [Chapter 7]

Not having any vital activity at all (i.e. not expending one's energies) is wiser than setting a great store on life and making attempts to lengthen it or preserve it (Chapter 75).

Like the later Taoist sects, which believed that magic

could make a man invulnerable, Lao Tzu affirms that there is no place for death in the Holy Man:

A man endowed with plentiful Te is comparable to a newborn infant: poisonous insects will not sting him, wild animals will not seize him in their claws, birds of prey will not carry him off in their talons; his bones are weak, his sinews supple, but his grasp is firm. He knows nothing about the union of the sexes, yet his little penis stands on end: what perfect concentration of spermatic energy! He can scream all day without getting hoarse: what perfection of harmony! He who knows harmony is permanent; he who knows how to be permanent is illumined [*ming*]. All excess of life is ill-omened; when the will attempts to control the breath, it makes it rigid. [Chapter 55]

We come out [of the Unseen] to be born and we reenter it to die. Three in ten of us are companions of life, and three in ten are companions of death. And the men who, though having life, rush toward death are also three in ten. Why? Because they live too intensely. I have heard that those who excel in maintaining their life principle do not fear rhinoceroses and tigers when traveling, and bear neither breastplates nor weapons in the army. In such a man there is no place for the rhinoceros to plunge its horn, the tiger to sink its claws, nor the warrior to thrust his blade. Why? Because in such a man there is no place for death. [Chapter 50]

The "companions of life" are those who have the suppleness and nonresistance of the newborn child, while the "companions of death" are those who are already as stiff and unbending as corpses (Chapter 76). The same general law holds for plant life. Too much rigidity or trust in one's strength is always an omen of defeat; men of violence never come to a natural end (Chapter 42).

So the suppleness and nonresistance that Lao Tzu advocates in politics find their application in the individual. To live long, the individual has to live wisely, i.e. according to the ideal of *wu-wei*, which will enable him, on the one hand, not to exhaust himself, and on the other, to foster the soft elasticity he was born with. Unfortunately, Lao Tzu gives few positive directives concerning the methods for achieving long life. He does hint, however, at one of the most important: breath control. This method, also referred to by Chuang Tzu, has always been one of the most commonly practiced techniques for prolonging life; it comprised numerous exercises of varying degrees of complexity. The following passage of the *Tao Te Ching* contains an allusion to a breath technique:

Let your bodily soul and your spiritual soul embrace the Unity, and you will be able to keep them from separating!

Concentrate your breath and make it supple, and you will be like an infant! Polish your spiritual mirror and you will make it faultless! Govern the people with consideration and you will be able to avoid intervening! Open and shut [as necessary] your heavenly gates [eyes, ears, and the other openings], and you will keep your femininity! Let your illumined mind penetrate every region of space and you will be able to renounce learning! [Chapter 10]

The Chinese believed in two souls, or rather two groups of souls or vital spirits, a Yang group (*hun*) and a Yin group (*p'o*). The *hun* governed the breath and the superior functions; the *p'o* were connected with the blood, the bones, and organic life in general. To maintain life and health, these two kinds of soul had to be joined harmoniously; if they separated, sickness and death resulted. "Embracing the unity" is the same as obtaining this physical wholeness; but the expression must also be taken in a mystical sense to mean embracing the Tao, which is the One and the principle of unity. This is why the quest for long life is no different from the quest for the Tao; physical and moral hygiene is a means of attaining holiness. We cannot be sure what the concentration of breath alluded to in the passage quoted above consisted of. It was probably some kind of breathing technique designed to retain the energies contained in the air one has breathed (*ch'i*) and to make the process perfectly free and silent, yet without any intervention of the will, for this might make the breath "rigid" (Chapter 55). "The spiritual mirror" is often used in Taoist literature as a metaphor for the "still" mind of the Holy Man, which gives a faithful reflection of all things.* The same idea is expressed in the last sentence: this mirror, this perfectly illumined mind, lights up the whole world as it reflects it. Holiness is an illumination purely from within.

MYSTICISM

Insofar as it discards discursive knowledge in favor of intuition, and asserts the possibility of reaching, through quietism, a superior reality, the thought of the *Tao Te Ching* is indeed a form of mysticism. Like all mystics, Lao Tzu never attempts to give a rational demonstration of his doctrine; his teachings are deliberately obscure and ambiguous, and they can often be interpreted on more than one level. Thus the warning against the senses and "maddening" sports (Chapter 12) can be taken as a mere moral exhortation; but it can also mean that asceticism is a prerequisite for long life; and on yet another level it can designate one of the steps leading to ecstasy. This state must in fact be prepared for by purifying the soul of everything extraneous to the Tao. The same complex idea seems to be expressed in Chapter 10 (quoted above) and in Chapter 52: "block the openings, shut the doors"; "after using its outer glitter, return to its inner light." Lao Tzu uses the word

* This theme is discussed in Paul Demiéville, "Le Miroir spirituel," *Sinologica*, Vol. I, No. 2 (1948), 112–37.

ming (light) on several occasions to mean the Holy Man's characteristic insight into the mysteries; but these mysteries are "darknesses full of light, which surpass our capacity for seeing and understanding."*

Lao Tzu, then, is a mystic. But to what extent is he a mystic? (For there are many degrees of mysticism, ranging from mere meditation to the ecstatic trance.) It is hard to form a sure opinion about Lao Tzu's mysticism. The *Lao Tzu* itself adds very little to our knowledge of Taoist mysticism. But fortunately we have the *Chuang Tzu,* a few significant passages of which will be given in the next chapter. The *Chuang Tzu* makes it clear that ecstatics were not rare among Taoists during the Period of the Philosophers. It portrays several personages in a state of trance, one of whom is none other than Lao Tan himself:

One day, Confucius went to visit the Taoist Holy Man.... He found him completely inert and looking like a lifeless body. Confucius had to wait for some time before he was able to address his host.

"Did my eyes deceive me?" he said. "Or was this really so? Just now, Sir, your body was like a piece of dry wood. You seemed to have left the world and men, and to have settled into an inaccessible solitude."

"Yes," replied Lao Tan, "I had gone for a stroll at the origin of all things." [*Chuang Tzu,* Chapter 21]

This anecdote, which certainly has no historical foundation, proves that the author considered Lao Tan to have experienced states of ecstasy. We can reasonably suppose that some such experience is behind certain remarks in the *Tao Te Ching.* Though the book gives no indication of the

* This remarkable phrase comes from a Western mystic, Mme Hélyot, as reported by Henri Bremond in his *Histoire littéraire du sentiment religieux en France,* V, 321 and quoted in Louis Bordet, *Religion et Mysticisme,* p. 24.

physical phenomena (catalepsy, etc.) that often, but not always, accompany ecstasy, it does contain many allusions and expressions that imply some experience of ecstatic states: immediate and all-embracing knowledge without reference to the senses, quietism, the obscurity of the Tao, the Unity that must be embraced (which might be an allusion to the mystical union), and so on. At the very least, we can suppose that the author had heard about mystical experiences from other members of his spiritual community.

In the passage cited above, Lao Tan's reply that he had gone to the "origin of all things" is remarkable for the way it sums up the main ideas of Taoist mysticism. The spiritual journey in question takes place in time rather than in space. The mystic returns to the beginning of all things, the Mother, the principle that existed before the gods, the invisible source of all life. No actual journey in time takes place, of course; the mystic abolishes time by identifying himself with an eternal now. Hence, being outside time, he can hope to avoid death.

But Lao Tzu does not believe in physical immortality: union with the Tao merely enables him to endure, to avoid dying prematurely (cf. Chapter 16, quoted on page 44). Nor does he believe in the survival of a personal soul. True, the *Tao Te Ching* is none too explicit on this score, but the fact that it does not put forward any differing opinion suggests that it subscribes to the view held by the other Taoists: seen creatures are merely the innumerable transitory forms adopted by the life that emerged from primordial chaos. These monads of life appear in this world as plants, animals, or human beings, then disappear into formlessness before reappearing in different guises. Thus something survives after death; but that something is as impersonal as can be imagined. On this issue also Chuang Tzu gives us a better understanding of the school's doctrine; we shall see that he considered life and death to be two aspects of the same phenomenon. Lao Tzu describes them as a coming-forth and a going-back, the law common to all creatures. But it seems that the Holy Man is able mystically to place himself outside this process by realizing within himself the perfect void that identifies him with the emptiness and utter simplicity of the Tao—in other words, by overcoming the multiplicity of our nature and embracing the Unity. Here all questions of life and death and the afterlife become irrelevant. The Holy Man's vital and spiritual principles, gathered into an indivisible unity, are free from all vicissitude and determinism; they no longer belong to this world. We might talk of an immortal soul, but the Taoists express themselves differently. To them, the immortal principle dwelling in the heart of the Holy Man is the Tao and none other. Hence there is no immortality other than that of the Tao itself.

Once again, however, Lao Tzu is not explicit about mystic experience; his doctrine is more concerned with how to make the best of our life in this world than with eschatology. This is why, while advocating a moderate form of asceticism, he suggests—or rather hints at—the advantages that the quietist attitude secures at various levels. To the ruler, he demonstrates that laissez-faire is the best method of government; but the ruler must further possess the Virtue of the Holy Men. For Te is a strength that is all-powerful (Chapter 59) and never failing (Chapter 28). The ruler who possessed it, as a true Taoist Holy Man, would have an occult power that his subjects would not even be aware of. If he could preserve quietude and simplicity in the likeness of the Tao, not only the nations, but all creatures would model themselves on natural harmony; by his perfect absence of desire and tranquil emptiness the Ruler–Holy Man would establish peace on earth. Thus mysticism, politics, and the quest for long life form a congruous set of interdependent disciplines; for everything is dependent on everything else in a monistic view of the universe.

INSIPIDITY OF THE TAO

Lao Tzu's calm, reflective mysticism makes no call upon the violent emotions. Nothing in the *Tao Te Ching* suggests that ecstatic dancing or other inducements to trance were resorted to. Nor is there any borrowing from the language of love to describe actual experiences. The only path to ecstasy seems to be a long cathartic meditation. Lao Tzu is fully aware of the initial unattractiveness of his doctrine:

> Music and fine food make the passerby pause.
> How different is that which the mouth utters about the Tao!
> How tasteless, how lacking in savor!
> For if you look at it, you can see nothing; if you listen to it, you find nothing to hear; if you use it, you can never use it up.
>
> [Chapter 35]

> When the superior man has heard of the Tao, he hastens to follow it.
> When the average man has heard of the Tao, he sometimes thinks about it, sometimes forgets it.
> When the inferior man hears of the Tao, he bursts out laughing: if he did not laugh, it would not really be the Tao.
> Hence the proverb has it:
> The illumined Tao seems obscure;
> The Tao that goes forward seems to go backward;
> The Tao that is smooth seems rough.
> The superior Te seems hollow like a valley.

The purest whiteness seems sullied.
The most abundant Te seems scanty;
The sturdiest Te seems fragile;
The most solid truth seems specious.
The greatest square has no corners,
The greatest vessel takes the longest to finish,
The greatest music cannot be heard.
The greatest image cannot be seen.
The Tao is hidden and nameless.
The Tao alone excels in beginning and finishing. [Chapter 41]

My words are very easy to understand and to put into practice, yet no one in the world is capable of understanding them and putting them into practice. . . . This is why the Holy Man dresses in homespun and hides a jade within his bosom. [Chapter 70]

If the Tao is insipid, the Taoist who, as it were, embodies it, is no less so, for the light that he bears within stays hidden; to be authentic, it must not be apparent to the vulgar. Not only must his holiness go unrecognized, but the true Taoist must, in his perfect simplicity, give the appearance of a fool:

While the crowd is feasting at a great sacrifice or going up to the terraces for the springtime festivities, I remain alone in impassive immobility, like an infant who has not yet learned how to smile.

I am like a homeless wretch. While the others have more than enough, I alone seem to have lost everything.

How stupid I look! How boorish!

How brilliant people are! I alone am dull.

How self-assured they are! I alone am vacillating.

They all have some particular talent, and I alone am as ignorant as a churl.

Different from the others, I alone prefer to suck my mother's breast. [Chapter 20]

CHUANG TZU

Most of the ancient quietist texts have been lost; apart from the *Lao Tzu*, almost all that is left us is the *Chuang Tzu*. We can include the *Lieh Tzu* also, despite its contested authenticity (the version we have appears to have been compiled in the third century A.D., whereas its supposed author, Lieh Yü-k'ou, lived in the fourth or the fifth century B.C.), for it contains elements of very early date and on this account remains quite interesting. Fragments of lost texts have been preserved in other works; but these sources are secondary compared with the three books whose supposed authors have been called the Fathers of Taoism. If the *Tao Te Ching* is by far the most famous, the *Chuang Tzu* is incontestably the most important; it, above all, gives us insight into the thought and the way of life of the early Taoists.

CHUANG CHOU

Little is known, unfortunately, about Chuang Chou, the author of the *Chuang Tzu*. The *Historical Memoirs* inform us that he came from the Sung dependency Meng, in what is now Honan. For a time, he served as a petty official at the Lacquer Garden (Ch'i-yüan); though the exact dates of his life are unknown, they seem to fall within the fourth century B.C. This is all the historian really knows; the biography that follows consists mainly of critical appreciations of his work. Chuang Chou, he tells us, was interested in all the intellectual movements of his day, but his preference tended toward the doctrine of Lao Tzu, and his writings generally give metaphorical illustrations of that doctrine. "He wrote excellently. His style was remarkably exact and lively. He used his talents to skewer the partisans of Confucius and Mo Tzu. The best scholars of the day were incapable of defending themselves from his onslaughts. He had a sparkling wit and no respect for anyone, with the result that nobody could make use of him, not even kings and princes." To illustrate this last remark, Ssu-ma Ch'ien tells the following anecdote:

King Wen of Ch'u, hearing of Chuang Tzu's talents, sent a messenger to him, bearing costly gifts, and inviting him to come to court as his minister. Chuang Tzu laughed and told the messenger from Ch'u: "A thousand pounds of gold make a handsome sum indeed; ministerhood is indeed very honorable. But have you ever seen the ox being led to the sacrifice? After being fattened up for several years, it is decked out in embroidered trappings and led into the great temple. At this moment it would undoubtedly prefer to be an uncared-for piglet, but it is too late, isn't it? Go away! Do not defile me! I would rather frolic joyously in the mire than be haltered by the ruler of a state. I will never take office. Thus I will remain free to live as I see fit."

This anecdote is the sole biographical detail to have survived. It crops up again in a slightly different form in the *Chuang Tzu* itself. Though its authenticity cannot be guaranteed, it does give some indication of the early Taoists' mentality. Like the hermit sages, they felt that any abrogation of their freedom or any compromise with the ruling powers would defile them.

THE SOPHIST HUI SHIH

We learn from the *Chuang Tzu* that Chuang Chou had formed a friendship with Hui Shih. Indeed, it is thanks to Chapter 33 of this book that the themes treated by this famous Sophist have been preserved.* Their friendship did not prevent them from quarreling fiercely about philosophical matters, however. These disputes were fine sport for Chuang Tzu's polemical wit, to judge from the numerous passages in which the two are seen at loggerheads. What the Taoist regretted after Hui Shih's death was not his death itself—that would have been against his principles—but the loss of stimulating opposition from an artful disputer:

Chuang Tzu once passed by the grave of Hui Shih. Turning to his attendants, he said: "There was once a plasterer who used to ask his friend, a stonemason, to chip off the bits of plaster, no thicker than a fly's wing, that dropped on to his nose. The stonemason would give a swish of his ax and the spot of plaster was gone, leaving the nose intact, without the least flinch from the plasterer. The prince of Sung, hearing of this, sent for the stonemason and asked him to try his trick before him. The stonemason replied: 'It's true that I can do this thing with an ax; unfortunately, the material that I used to work upon is dead.' Since the Master's death, I too have been without material to practice upon. I have no one left to argue with." [Chapter 24]

So the fact that Hui Shih's doctrine is known to us through the *Chuang Tzu* is no mere chance. His paradoxes are very interesting, despite their obscurity, for they imply a background of logical, not to say scientific, investigation

* Kou Pao-koh, *Deux Sophistes Chinois: Houei Che et Kong-Souen Long* (Paris, 1953).

about which we know nothing. As Fung Yu-lan remarks,* only the conclusions of the discussions are given, and Chapter 33 (T'ien-hsia) says nothing at all about their premises. Yet this chapter, while criticizing Hui Shih, gives us a glimpse of an inquisitive mind interested in all kinds of problems and highly characteristic of its period. "He was a man of many skills and could argue a point of view about everything.... When asked why the sky did not fall and why the earth did not sink, and whence came wind, rain, and thunder, Hui Shih never dodged the question; he had an answer for everything without even bothering to think." But his governing idea was that the Universe is One, with the corollary that all creatures must be loved universally. Here Hui Shih comes close to Mo Tzu's doctrine of universal love; but, as has been pointed out, Mo Tzu is thinking exclusively of men, whereas Hui Shih extends love to include all creatures, and bases it on the metaphysical idea of the identity of opposites. Thus Hui Shih goes beyond Mo Ti's humanism and approaches Lao Tzu's Immensity (*ta*) and Unity (*i*) of the Tao.

Among Hui Shih's paradoxes in the T'ien-hsia chapter, we find these definitions of Unity, which he uses to justify the identification of the notions of size: "The infinitely great, beyond which there is nothing, I call Great One (*ta-i*); the infinitely small, within which there is nothing, I call Small One (*hsiao-i*)." "One" signifies both unity and totality; therefore the expressions Great One and Small One imply the idea that the whole is present in both the immense and the minute, in the cosmos and the cheese mite.

Apart from this, Hui Shih's paradoxes express an abso-

* Quoted in *Deux Sophistes Chinois*, p. 95.

lute relativism that aims at disparaging common ideas about qualities and the nature of things, and about space and time. This Sophist relativism differs from that of Lao Tzu, whose main aim was to give standing to his idea of tolerant wisdom and to his mysticism. Let us quote a few of these Sophisms, which, as we shall see, influenced Chuang Tzu:

> That which has no thickness cannot be piled up, yet can cover a thousand *li*.
> Heaven and earth are equally low; mountain and marsh are equally flat.
> The sun at noon is the sun setting; when a creature is born, it dies.
> . . . The middle of the world is north of Yen and south of Yüeh.*

Another famous Sophist, Kung-sun Lung, was also a contemporary of Chuang Tzu, but younger. He is known for his treatises on the "white horse that is not a horse" and on the "separation of the hard and the white," though these paradoxes were not of his invention. However, Kung-sun Lung's philosophical position is quite different from Hui Shih's and Chuang Tzu's. The latter deny differences, affirming instead the fundamental unity of things, whereas Kung-sun Lung pursues the opposite aim of "rectifying the denominations," as Confucius put it—bringing words into line with realities. This led him to carry logical analysis to the point of paradox.

Thus Hui Shih and Chuang Tzu, despite their differences of opinion, were on the same side of the fence so far as metaphysics was concerned, and probably each influenced the other. For all that, Chuang Tzu is unvaryingly hostile toward Sophistry; any borrowings he makes from it—rela-

---

* Yen was the northernmost state in ancient China, and Yüeh the southernmost. A commentator explains this by saying that the world is infinitely great, so its middle is everywhere.

tivist arguments or rhetorical techniques—are confined to the negative part of his teachings, the critique of values.

THE EQUALITY OF THINGS AND OPINIONS

The bulk of the second chapter of the *Chuang Tzu* is given up to a critique of common judgments and opinions. If we start from the principle that all things and creatures (men included) are fundamentally identical, i.e. are one, then we cannot legitimately pass judgment on them; we cannot approve of some and condemn others. Confrontations of opposed sets of opinions take place when people have lost their sense of universality: each side is blind to all but its own small parcel of self-interested truths, which it takes for the absolute. "The Tao is hidden by small achievements," i.e. by the closed systems into which petty minds shut themselves and would presume to shut others. However, as Lao Tzu demonstrates, affirmations and negations never fail to give rise to one another: if I am right, my neighbor must be wrong, and since my neighbor is equally convinced that he is right and I am wrong, the evil is without a cure; for we each cling to our own sets of prejudices. Granted, men apparently differ in character, temperament, and intelligence. This means that we each have a particular self that we oppose to the selves of others. Yet within each of us there is a "Supreme Master" superior to all these distinctive particularisms, which arise from our viscera; but since it cannot be perceived by the senses, we have difficulty in believing it exists. Whether or not we believe in it, however, neither adds to nor detracts from its reality. This Supreme Master is, of course, the Tao, the principle of life and unity, which the Taoists saw as a superior, impersonal soul. The trouble is that in most of us the

Supreme Ruler is obscured by passion and prejudice. And, what is just as bad, we use words to express opinions and to outshine our fellows—sterile strife that not only creates divisions between men, but exhausts the vital energies and spirituality of each one. "They sink into their actions as into deep water, from which no one can retrieve them. . . . These minds are almost dead; nothing can restore them to the light."

Faced with this sorry spectacle, what attitude is the Taoist to take? Naturally, he cannot let himself get drawn into these endless disputes. He lets himself be illumined by Heaven, the source of that inner light which, for Chuang Tzu as for Lao Tzu, is the sign of holiness; he never pushes himself to the fore nor does he pit himself against reality. Having recognized the radical relativity of the notions of good and evil, true and false—knowing, for instance, that each of the doctrines that claims a following for itself (Confucius's and Mo Tzu's in particular) is an inextricable complex of affirmations and negations—the Holy Man is so neutral, so empty, that he offers no resistance to any would-be opponent, whether a person or an idea. In this way he identifies himself with what Chuang Tzu calls "the axis of the Tao": somewhat like the pivot of a compass, he is at the center of a circle. Here, once again, is the symbol of the hub, the center of a wheel, so often used by Taoist authors. Huai-nan Tzu affirms that by "grasping the axis of the Tao," the Sage can go wandering in the realm of the infinite.

In this chapter of the *Chuang Tzu*, however, the infinity in question is not mystical infinity but, as the text itself explains, the vicious circle of opinions. The Sage's impartiality enables him to place himself at the center of the ring of contradictions and let them wind past indefinitely without his replying to one or another of them in particular. This is an application of Lao Tzu's ideal of *wu-wei* and non-resistance. Placing oneself at the center of the ring does not imply any purely negative attitude toward the world, however; the Sage does not go off into a morose retirement to avoid being defiled by real life. This was not Lao Tzu's attitude—his wish was to share the defilement. Neither is it Chuang Tzu's—he had no scorn for any creature, judged no one, and accepted the customs of his age (Chapter 33). "A road [*tao*] is made by the people who walk on it": the validity of a sound or word to describe a particular object is determined by usage. Since all is one to the Sage, he will keep to custom and not go around imposing his own whims as universal norms. On the contrary, even though men's preferences appear ridiculous to him, he will be like the monkey trainer who, obliged to cut down on his animals' daily rations, announced: "You'll get three measures in the morning and four at night." This made all the monkeys furious. "Well, then," he said, "you'll get four in the morning and three at night." The monkeys were all delighted (Chapter 2). Since conflict is always due to the shortsightedness of human beings, who are not much better than impassioned monkeys, the Taoist resolves the discord by sheer disinterest. Having no preference for one solution over another, he could not care less which one will carry the day.

So much for our outline of the first part of Chapter 2 (Ch'i-wu-lun), which ends as follows:

Beyond the limits of the world the Holy Man exists, yet does not theorize; within the limits of the world, the Holy Man theorizes yet does not criticize. In the *Spring and Autumn Annals*, a book intended to school the age and to set forth the ideas of the ancient rulers, the Holy Man criticizes but does not argue. You want to discriminate? Some things cannot be discriminated among. You want to argue? Some things cannot be argued about. So what is to be done? The Holy Man embraces everything. People who argue do so for show. That is why I say: When you argue, there are some things you are failing to see. In the greatest Tao, nothing is named; in the greatest disputation, nothing is said; greatest benevolence is not benevolent; greatest humility is not humble; greatest bravery is not aggressive. If the Tao turns to brilliance, it is no longer the Tao; if speech turns to disputation, it no longer achieves its aim; if benevolence becomes a habit, it is no longer perfect; if humility turns into affectation, it is hypocrisy; if bravery turns to aggression, it ceases to prevail. These five qualities degenerate from universality into pettiness; therefore the best thing is to stop within the scope of cognition. Who knows how to employ disputation without words, the Tao without name? He who could do so would possess a heavenly treasury. Pour into it and it is never full, dip from it and it never runs dry; yet no one would know where this wealth came from. This is what I call the Restrained Light.

There is a single reality hidden behind the diversity of things and creatures. We stray from that reality, we sin, as soon as we start delimiting and fastening on partial aspects of reality. The great moral failing of the sectarians and the disputers is to keep rigidly to a single point of view.

Discursive knowledge is condemned, therefore, as in Lao Tzu, for it cannot help being partial, incomplete, and false. From the Taoist point of view, it is even dangerous, for all it does is use up the most precious and sacred asset of all: life. "Our life is limited, but knowledge is limitless: It is dangerous to pursue the limitless with limited capabilities; hence the man who strives for knowledge is nothing less than rash" (Chapter 3). We must "be content with what we know" and not let ourselves be drawn into an endless chase. The only valid knowledge is all-embracing and intuitive. "Men who cultivated the Tao in former times fostered their learning with quietude. When knowledge made its appearance, they did not use it in order to act; it can be said that they used it solely in order to foster their quietude" (Chapter 16). Absolute tranquillity and learning must, so to speak, foster one another; this kind of learning is not knowledge of detail, but knowledge of the whole, independent of the senses. The senses yield only points of view, mere aspects of reality, and what is worse, they give rise to desire and passion. Perfect knowledge is of a mystical nature; it effaces even the distinction between the subjective self and the objective self. "Heaven and Earth were born with me, and the Ten Thousand Creatures are one with me." But this is true solely from the point of view of the Tao and the mystic who does not speak, because (according to a passage in Chapter 2) as soon as I posit unity I destroy it, since my affirmation itself is enough to create a duality. Chuang Tzu probably means that the cause of multiplicity in being is the self. Hence true unity exists only for the ecstatic. This is the gist of the following extract also, which gives a good summary of the doctrine in question:

Knowledge traveled north along the banks of the Mysterious River; he climbed a hill that loomed up in the shadows and met the Silent One. "I have a few questions to put to you," he said. "By what meditation, by what cogitation, may I know the Tao? In what place, following what practices, may I rest in the Tao? By what school and what way may I obtain the Tao?" To these three questions, the Silent One made no reply. Not that he would not, but that he could not.

When Knowledge got no reply, he went back south to the White River and climbed up Foxhole Mountain; he caught sight of the Jester, to whom he put the same questions. "Wait, now. I know. I'll tell you. . . ." But just as he was about to speak, the Jester forgot what he wanted to say.

When Knowledge got no reply, he went back to the ruler's palace; there he found Huang Ti, to whom he put the same questions. Huang Ti replied: "Don't meditate, don't cogitate, and then you will know the Tao. Don't bother with the place or the practices, and then you will rest in the Tao. Follow no school, follow no way, and then you will attain the Tao."

Knowledge said to Huang Ti: "You know it and I know it, but these two do not. Who is right?"

Huang Ti replied: "The Silent One is genuinely right, and the Jester is close to being right. You and I are wholly wrong. For he who knows does not speak; he who speaks does not know. This is why the Holy Man freely dispenses a teaching without words. The Tao does not appear on command; Te is not acquired at will. It is possible to practice benevolence or fall into righteousness and the rites, which is going from one sham to another. This is why it is written: When the Tao falls into disuse, virtue arises; when virtue falls into disuse, humanheartedness arises; when humanheartedness falls into disuse, righteousness arises; when righteousness falls into disuse, ritualism arises. The rites are but the glitter of the Tao and the beginning of anarchy. This is why it is said: He who practices the Tao diminishes his glitter every day; by diminishing and diminishing he attains the state of inaction; in this state of inaction, there is nothing he cannot do. That which has already attained the state of being—how difficult it is for it to go back to its root [the Tao]. It is easy for the Great Man alone. Life is the companion of death; death is the leader of life, but who knows their law? The life of a man is merely gathered breath [*ch'i*]. When it is gathered, there is life; when it disperses, there is death. Since life and death are each other's companion, why worry about them? All creatures are one. The life they love seems like marvelous vitality to them; the death they hate, foul putrefaction. But this putrefaction turns back into vitality, and vitality turns back into putrefaction. This is why we should say: In this world, there is one and only one breath of life, and the Holy Man venerates the One." [Chapter 22]

IDENTITY OF LIFE AND DEATH

Chuang Tzu's intuition of a universe that is fundamentally one enables him to contemplate the problem of life and death with great serenity of mind. Life and death are merely two aspects of the same reality, and the change from one to the other is as natural as the succession of day and night, waking and sleeping. The same theme had already been touched on by Lao Tzu, but Chuang Tzu develops it and illustrates it in one of the most famous passages in the book:

When Chuang Tzu's wife died, Hui Tzu went along to offer his condolences. He found Chuang Tzu squatting on the ground, singing and beating time on a bowl. Hui Tzu said: "Not to shed a tear over the corpse of your partner in life, the mother of your children and your companion in growing old—that would be bad enough. But to sing away, drumming on a bowl, is just going too far!"

"Not at all," replied Chuang Tzu. "When she died, I could not help being affected at first. But, reflecting on the origin of all being, I discovered that there was a time when she was not yet born, when she was not even a physical creature. There was even a time when she was not a breath: she was mingled with the nebulousness of Chaos. From this state a first change gave the breath; a further change gave a corporeal foundation [to the breath]; and a final change gave the body life. And now, by virtue of yet another change, she is dead. These phases are like the sequence of the four seasons, from spring to autumn, from summer to winter. She is asleep now, untroubled in the Great Resting Place. For me to start weeping and wailing would be to proclaim myself incapable of understanding destiny, and that is why I refrain." [Chapter 18]

Life and death are nothing more than natural metamorphoses, mere transmutations of forms, such as the transformation of silkworms into bombyx moths. But ancient peasant beliefs lingering on in the world of learning held the phenomenon to be much more general. The earliest almanacs taught that sparrows changed into oysters in the fall, and oysters into sparrows in the spring. The assumption underlying the *I Ching* is that all phenomena and events interchange permutationally, and can be foretold from the symbolic mutations which a specialist in the diagrams can decipher. On a more concrete level, both the *Chuang Tzu* and the *Lieh Tzu* give a list of creatures that change into each other. Unfortunately, this important passage is untranslatable, since nobody these days knows the exact meaning of the names of the animals and plants that it refers to. We can, however, give the introductory fable:

When traveling one day, Lieh Tzu stopped to eat at the roadside, and his eyes fell upon a skull nearly a hundred years old. Clearing away the brambles, he addressed it as follows: "Only you and I know that there is no such thing as life and death. Are you really the wretch, and am I the fortunate one? A seed develops according to the circumstances of time and place in which it finds itself: when it finds water, it becomes a [microorganism called] *chi*."

[*Chuang Tzu*, Chapter 18; *Lieh Tzu*, Chapter 1]

The text ends with a list of a series of transformations that result in man, who "goes back into the great weaving machine: thus all creatures issue from the Loom and return to the Loom."

In another passage, Chuang Tzu puts words into the mouth of a dead man whose skull he has found:

Chuang Tzu was on his way to the kingdom of Ch'u, when he saw an empty skull, fleshless but intact. Striking it with his riding whip, he said: "Was it losing your wits in your lust for life that brought you to this? Or were you sent to the block because you ruined your country? Or did you act wrongly and shower shame on your parents, wife, and children? Or was it owing to poverty, cold, and hunger? Or did old age bring you to this pass?" On saying these words, he picked up the skull and used it as a pillow for his sleep.

At midnight, the skull appeared to him in a dream, and said: "You speak like a Sophist. Everything you say concerns the problems of the living. These things do not exist for the dead. Would you like to hear about the dead?"

"Gladly," said Chuang Tzu.

The skull went on: "Among the dead, there are no such things as lords, vassals, seasons, or tasks. Peaceful as we are, we have no age but that of Heaven and Earth. A king on his throne does not enjoy greater felicity than ours."

Incredulous, Chuang Tzu asked: "If I prevailed upon the Governor of Destinies to restore life to your body, together with your bones, flesh, and skin, to bring back your father, mother, wife, children, and childhood friends, would you not be willing?"

The skull stared at him with its empty eye sockets, frowned, and said: "Why should I give up my kingly felicity and return to human misery?" [*Chuang Tzu*, Chapter 18]

In Chuang Tzu, death is generally presented as a natural phenomenon that we ought neither to fear nor to desire. In this fable, however, he comes around to suggesting that the dead are better off than the living. This is a fairly foreseeable culmination of his doctrine, for as soon as men admit the fact of an afterlife, they are invariably led to imagine it in a happier light than their life in this world. True, the paradises often have their counterparts, the hells; but before Buddhism gained influence, the ancient Chinese had no image of hell. There is a contradiction, nonetheless, between the materialistic conception of the physical metamorphoses of creatures and the conception of another life after death. Chuang Tzu does not seem to be bothered by this contradiction, which is probably only apparent. Although he does not say so explicitly, his positing of spiritual survival excludes the survival of a personal soul. When he puts words into the mouth of the ghost in his dream, he is merely using a popular belief to illustrate his theme that death is not necessarily fearsome. Chuang Tzu's real attitude is primarily a resigned, not to say joyful, acceptance of our destiny.

Tzu Lai was ill and at the point of giving up his last breath. His wife and children gathered round him in tears. Tzu Li, who had come to ask how he was, shooed them away, saying: "Do not disturb the process of the Transformation!"

Then, leaning against the doorpost, he addressed Tzu Lai. "Great is the working of the Creator! What is he going to make of you now? Where is he going to lead you? Will he turn you into a rat's liver? An insect's arm?"

Tzu Lai said: "A child owes obedience to his parents whether they send him east or west, north or south. The Yin and the Yang are much more than parents to us. Now that they are bringing me to the threshold of death, if I were to rebel, I would be nothing less than perverse. How could I bear them a grudge? The immense mass of the universe gave me a body for my dwelling, a lifetime for my labors, an old age for my ease, and death for my rest. So the same reasons bring us to think well of both life and death. When an ironfounder is at work, if the metal should leap up and say, 'I insist on being made into the Mo-yeh sword,' he would surely regard it as inauspicious metal. Now, having had a human form bestowed upon me, if I were to shout, 'I don't want to be anything but a man!' the Great Creator would surely regard me as a most inauspicious man." [Chapter 6]

When Chuang Tzu was at the point of death, his disciples expressed a wish to give him a splendid funeral. But Chuang Tzu said: "Heaven and Earth are my coffin and my grave; for burial regalia, I will have the sun and moon as my double jade ring, the stars as my jewels; and I will have the Ten Thousand Creatures to escort me. As you can see, nothing will be lacking for the ceremony; what would you add to this?"

The disciples replied: "We fear that you may be eaten by the crows and kites, Master."

Chuang Tzu replied: "Above ground, I will be eaten by the crows and kites; below, I will be eaten by the crickets and ants. Why rob one to feed the other? What partiality!" [Chapter 32]

CHUANG TZU'S MYSTICISM

Like his predecessor, Lao Tzu, who had denounced the perversion of the human mind by intellect and civilization, Chuang Tzu sets out to purify the soul by making it aware of the relativity of all social values. However, the ultimate aim behind his critique is to empty the concepts of life and death, to make people see them for what they really are: on the level of phenomena, "life" and "death" are merely changes of form. Questions regarding the existence of God and the immortality of the soul are not, it seems, really raised; on these points Chuang Tzu shows himself to be resolutely agnostic.

The insufficiency of human reason for the task of piercing the mystery of the universe is a major theme of the work. In Chapter 25, for instance, the author has two imaginary characters discuss the origin of the universe. One of them explains that the visible world is made up of the Yin and the Yang and the aggregate of the paired opposites, but that at this point human reason stops short. Then, during the discussion of whether a Prime Mover exists, one of them says:

"The dog barks and the cock crows: these things are familiar to everybody. Yet the wisest of us could not express this phenomenon in words, nor foresee what these animals intend to do. But let us analyze the real: let us go as far as the smallest conceivable particle; then let us think of an immeasurable immensity. To speak of an originating activity or to deny a creating activity is surely to remain the prisoner of contingent things and to end up in error. If I say: 'There is a Prime Mover,' it is because I am considering only that which is tangible. If I say: 'There is no creating activity,' it is because I am considering only that which is void and unseen. To limit oneself to that which has a name and a tangible existence is to remain in the domain of perceptible things; to discourse upon that which has no name and no tangible existence is to form a conception only of the vacuity of things. We can speak and think of these problems, but the more one speaks, the farther off the mark one gets. We cannot keep an unborn creature from being born, neither can we bring back a creature that is already dead. Life and death are not alien to us, and yet their principle is hidden from us. To speak of the existence or absence of a Prime Mover is nothing less than rationalizing from ignorance. I consider the origins: they run away into a limitless past. I seek the ends: they run up from the depths of an endless future. In this 'limitless' and this 'endless,' all discourse cancels out, participating in the essence of all creatures; and as to the problem of the existence or absence of a Prime Mover, it is the starting point for the discourse that thenceforth participates in the destiny common to all transitory creatures.

The Tao cannot be affirmed to exist or not to exist. The name Tao is merely an artifice for practical purposes. Hence, whether there is or is not a Prime Mover, the question can have a meaning for the detail of things, but whatever could this mean for the Great Whole? If speech were really adequate, it would exhaust the problem of the Tao in a single day; but since it is not so, it can just about exhaust in a day whatever concerns a creature or a thing. The Tao is something beyond seen creatures; neither speech nor silence can convey it. Let us banish both speech and silence: we have reached the farthest limit of thought." [Chapter 25]

The questions of the origin of things and the existence of a creator are both dismissed as being irrelevant to the absolute. It is interesting to note, nonetheless, that such problems were in fact discussed, for they also raise the question of the immanence or transcendence of the Tao. But unfortunately we know nothing about the possible arguments for and against these theses. Chuang Tzu himself is unwilling to get involved in the debate, but a partially corrupt passage in Chapter 22 shows him to incline toward immanentism. A nuisance is bothering him with the pointless question: "Where is this thing you call Tao?" Chuang Tzu gives a succession of replies: "Tao is in an ant, a blade of grass, a tile, a manure heap." . . . "Don't try to determine it, for you'll never find it anywhere outside creatures." Hence the Tao is immanent: its infinity is present at the core of things; it is their principle of unity and intelligibility, and also the principle of their inherent being and their efficacy, their Te.

But it would be wrong to take this Westernized interpretation of Chuang Tzu's thought too far. If the Tao is present at the core of things, it is also exterior to them, above them, and anterior to them: it is an autonomous reality in its own right. This is why it has to be "obtained."

In the Tao there is reality and efficacy, but it neither acts nor has form: you can receive it, but not grasp it;* you can obtain it, but not see it. It is trunk and root in itself. Before Heaven and Earth existed, it had existed for all eternity. It gives the spirits of the dead and the royal ancestors their sacred power; it gives life to Heaven and Earth. [Chapter 6]

In this passage, and in many others, Chuang Tzu uses the same terms as Lao Tzu. He goes on to refer to the mythological heroes who owed their exploits to the Tao they had "obtained." But if everything we do is not crowned with success, it is because civilization and its artifices cloud our awareness of the Tao. We hunt it out, even, and it takes flight from our impure souls, overflowing as they are with desire and passion. Hence we must empty our "hearts" for the Tao to come and dwell in them: in other words, holiness comes through a purification of the soul by a progressive ascetic discipline.

The *Chuang Tzu* and the *Lieh Tzu* contain several allusions, in the form of anecdotes, to the cathartic process that

* In this phrase I have adopted a textual correction made by Wen I-to.

the Taoists, and all other mystics, consider an indispensable preliminary to illumination. In the following passage from the *Lieh Tzu*, we can also see the workings of a typical master-pupil relationship. Lieh Tzu had come home "riding the wind" from a period of instruction with a master. A disciple came along in the hope of being initiated into this art of wind-riding. But he waited in vain for several months without Lieh Tzu's ever speaking to him, so he eventually went away, but returned some time afterward. Lieh Tzu then addressed him as follows:

"Sit down and I'll tell you what I learned from my master. Three years after I had begun to serve him, my mind no longer dared to distinguish between true and false, and my mouth no longer dared to speak about useful and harmful; then, for the first time, I got a look from my master. After five years, my mind again started distinguishing between true and false, and my mouth again started speaking about useful and harmful; then, for the first time, my master's face brightened and he smiled. After seven years, I managed to free my thoughts of all notions of true and false; I managed to free my speech of useful and harmful. Then, for the first time, the master invited me to sit beside him on his mat. After nine years, I managed to give free rein to my mind and mouth; I was no longer aware of any truth or falsehood, any usefulness or harmfulness, that could concern myself or others, nor of having a master or of having a fellow disciple. Outside and inside were one, and my eyes were like my ears, my ears like my nose, my nose like my mouth—all my senses were alike. I felt as if my mind was solidifying, my body coming apart, and my bones and flesh dissolving. I no longer felt that my body leaned against something, nor that my feet touched the ground, but let myself be borne east and west by the wind, like a leaf or dry wood-shaving; and finally I could no longer tell whether I was carrying the wind along or whether the wind was carrying me." [*Lieh Tzu*, Chapter 2]

The Taoist master teaches in silence; the disciple has to understand intuitively what is expected of him. He slowly empties his mind and draws closer and closer to the master. In a final stage, however, when the adept reaches the state of ecstasy, even the master must disappear from his awareness.

Before the disciple can begin this course of silent instruction, he has to purify his mind. The ill-prepared disciple, who gives in to the trial of silence or believes he knows everything before it is really the case, is a frequent theme in Taoist literature. Experience soon proves to him that he was presumptuous. He then has to go back home, or go off to some desert place as a hermit. Sometimes the retreat is definitive. The same Lieh Tzu, Chuang Tzu tells us, went back home after his master had convinced him of his insufficiency:

For three years he did not go out. He did the cooking for his wife and fed his pigs as respectfully as if they had been men. He took no part in affairs; he did away with his artificial ornaments and returned to natural simplicity. He became like a clod of earth; in the midst of distraction he remained concentrated, and so on until the end of his life. [*Chuang Tzu*, Chapter 7]

In another passage, Confucius himself turns hermit. (He frequently crops up in the *Chuang Tzu*, sometimes mocked, sometimes cited as an example.) "Confucius took leave of his friends, dismissed his disciples, and retired to a great marsh, where he dressed himself in skins and haircloth and fed on acorns and chestnuts. He passed among the beasts without bothering them and among the birds without disturbing their activities" (Chapter 20).

A disciple worthy of receiving the Tao and of progressing mystically can come under the supervision of a master; but the master himself need not necessarily have experienced all the phases of the carthartic process:

Nan-po Tzu-k'uei asked Nü-yü: "How is it that, despite your age, you have the complexion of a child?"

"I have learned what the Tao is," replied Nü-yü.

"Can the Tao be studied?" asked Nan-po Tzu-k'uei.

"No," replied Nü-yü, "you aren't the proper man for that. Pu-liang I, now, was all disposed to be a Holy Man, but he didn't have the principle [Tao] for it, whereas I had the principle without being disposed. I wanted to teach him, hoping that he would indeed become a Holy Man; I thought that it would be easy to communicate the principle of holiness to someone who was already disposed. Taking him aside, I gave him some explanations and watched him. After three days, he managed to expel the world from his awareness. I kept on watching him: after seven days, he managed to expel the things near to him. I kept on watching him: after nine days, he managed to expel his own existence; when he had expelled his own existence, he saw himself illumined by a dawn. When he was illumined by the dawn, he had the vision of oneness; after the vision of oneness, he had no more past or present; when he had no more past or present, he entered the realm where there is no life and no death." [Chapter 6]

During the period of instruction, the master seems to be wholly passive, as required by the doctrine of *wu-wei* and the teaching without words. It is the adept himself who has to progress, gradually emptying himself of his social self. The master's role must have been to control the pace of the ascension to perfect ecstasy. As we have just seen, the ascension proceeded in stages—three, seven, and nine days, months, or years. He also intervened at the start of the initiation with a critique of conventional values and prejudices intended to free the thought processes. So reflection plays an important role in the early stages, but becomes irrelevant once illumination has been acquired; its purpose is to empty the mind of its clutter of opinions.

Any spiritual progression must start with the realization

that any activity whatever that is directed toward the exterior world—even as the result of distraction—can unleash a fatal series of reactions. This truth does not necessarily have to be revealed by an instructor: experience is still the best guide, and it can lead to sudden conversions. This is what happened to Chuang Tzu himself, according to the following anecdote:

When Chuang Tzu was strolling in the park of Tiao-ling, he saw a strange bird that came from the south. Its wings had a span of seven feet, and its eyes were an inch across. It brushed past Chuang Tzu's forehead and settled in a chestnut grove. Chuang Tzu said: "What kind of bird is this? With such strong wings it does not fly away. With such large eyes it does not see me." He picked up his skirts and ran toward it.

As he lay in wait, with his crossbow to hand, he saw a cicada that had found a nice place in the shade and was consequently quite forgetful of its safety: a mantis raised its pincers and attacked it, the sight of this prey making it quite forgetful of its own body. The strange bird thereupon took advantage of the opportunity to pounce upon them both, thereby forgetting its own nature. Chuang Tzu shot it down. He sighed: "Alas! how creatures wrong each other; in both these cases, they brought misfortune down upon themselves. And, throwing down his crossbow, he turned away. The gamekeeper pursued him with insults.

Once back home, Chuang Chou did not go down into his courtyard for three months. Lan Chü then asked him: "Master, why have you not been down to your courtyard for such a long time?"

Chuang Chou replied: "Until now I had always watched out for my body while forgetting my real safety; I had gazed on muddy water taking it for a clear spring. I learned from my master that when mingling with the vulgar, you have to behave like the vulgar. Now, when strolling in the park of Tiao-ling, I forgot my real safety. A strange bird brushed past my forehead, settled in a chestnut grove, and forgot its nature. The gamekeeper insulted me. That is why I have not been down to my courtyard." [Chapter 20]

This adventure made Chuang Tzu realize the danger of passion, which disturbs the soul, making it resemble muddied water when it ought to be still and clear. The Taoists held that the Holy Man's mind should be so quiet and apathetic that it resembles a mirror—the "mirror of Heaven and Earth that reflects the multiplicity of things" (Chapter 13). Lao Tzu had already urged us to polish our spiritual mirror; Chuang Tzu compares a mind rid of passion to calm, limpid water, "so clear that it reflects even the hairs of the beard and eyebrows" (Chapter 13).

Properly speaking, all that the mystical purification does is bring us back to our natural condition (or as Chuang Tzu puts it, our heavenly condition); for the Taoists held the human soul to be calm and passive by nature. The *Huai-nan Tzu* states that Heavenly Order, destroyed by the attractions of the exterior world, can be regained by adopting an apathetic detachment:

Man is naturally quiet; this is the nature he receives from Heaven. Under the influence of things, movement occurs in him; this is a deterioration of his nature. His soul responds to the things that present themselves, and his knowledge is thus set in motion. His knowledge puts him in touch with things, and love and hate are thus born in him—love and hate that give body to things—and this knowledge drawn outward can no longer come back to itself. This is how the Heavenly Order is destroyed in man. Those who are initiated into the Tao do not exchange the Heavenly for the Human.

[*Huai-nan Tzu*, Chapter 1]

Having purified his innermost being of its defilement—hence becoming like a mirror—and having regained his native simplicity (*p'u*) and unity, the adept is inhabited by the Tao and is no longer any different from the Tao. Outwardly, this union makes the adept seem absent, or rather, present in body alone while his soul is absent. We have already quoted the passage about Lao Tzu's trance, in which he explains that he had gone for a stroll at the origin of all things. The second chapter of the *Chuang Tzu* ("The Equality of Things and Opinions") opens on a man in a trance who, like Lao Tzu, seems to be in a state of catalepsy:

Nan-kuo Tzu-ch'i sat leaning on a stool, breathing softly, and gazing up at the sky; there he was, all discomposed, as if he had lost one half of himself. "What is the meaning of this?" asked Yen Ch'eng Tzu-yu, who was close by. "Is it really possible to give the body this appearance of dead wood and the soul this insensibility of dead ashes?"

And in another chapter, a disciple falls into a trance while his master is addressing him:

Nieh Ch'üeh put questions to P'ei I about the Tao. P'ei I replied: "Keep full control of your body, have but a single gaze, and the heavenly harmony will come and find you. Keep back your knowledge, unify your Self, and the spirit will come and dwell within you. Te will provide beauty for you, the Tao will be a dwelling for you. You will have the innocence of a newborn calf and you will ask no questions."

By the time P'ei I had finished speaking, Nieh Ch'üeh had dropped off to sleep. P'ei I went off singing joyfully:

> His body is like dead wood,
> His body is like dead ashes!
> There he is with perfect knowledge.
> He no longer troubles himself about contingencies.
> He is far away, plunged into darkness.
> He has lost consciousness and cannot be spoken to—
>   what manner of man is that?

[Chapter 22]

While appearing prostrate and absent, the ecstatic feels as if he has got free from gravity and is floating through the air: this is what Chuang Tzu calls "Spiritual Wandering" (the title of his first chapter). It is also the title of a famous poem: "Faraway Wandering."

SPIRITUAL WANDERING

Legend has it that Lieh Tzu could ride the wind: from the text that we have just been looking at, we can see that what was really involved was a journey of the mind. Belief in magical journeys through the air, whether on the wind or on some kind of miraculous steed, was no doubt widespread in Taoist circles. Chuang Tzu also refers to Lieh Tzu's feat of riding the wind, which he admires as the sign of an advanced state of holiness, a holiness that is still imperfect, however, for the wandering of the soul is independent of all contingencies, even the wind: "But as for those who let themselves be borne away by the unadulterated energies of Heaven and Earth [pure Yin and Yang] and can harness the six composite energies to rove through the limitless, whatever could they henceforth depend on?" (Chapter I).

This means that the Holy Man lives in perfect symbiosis with the cosmos; his life rhythm is so completely identified with the rhythm of the great forces of nature (the Yin and the Yang and their compounds, which are manifest in the seasons, in the weather, and in creatures generally) that it is indistinguishable from them, and hence participates in the infinity and immortality of nature. For in that infinity and immortality lies life in its truest sense, quite distinct from ordinary biological life with its counterpart, death. In view of this, the Taoist philosophers had nothing but scorn for the majority of the physiological techniques for prolonging life indefinitely. They held that the only true immortality lay in the Tao, and no doubt conceived of it as permanent ecstasy. Chuang Tzu refers to a marvelous land inhabited by a kind of demigods or supermen, who are in some way the model of behavior to which the Holy Man must aspire. Like Lieh Tzu, "they are borne through the air and the clouds, their carriages are drawn by flying dragons. . . . They roam beyond the four seas [i.e. extraspatially]; their spiritual potency has solidified" (Chapter 1). This last phrase is important, for it refers to the essential feature of the Taoist spiritual technique, consisting of freezing the faculties of the soul, concentrating them in a single point. This is the equivalent of Lao Tzu's precept: Embrace the Unity, and empty your mind of its clutter of ideas. The adept who attains this perfect vacuity is godlike:

The Perfect Man is pure spirit. He feels neither the heat of the blazing brushlands nor the cold of the flooding waters; the light-ning that splits the mountains and the tempest that stirs up the ocean cannot frighten him. A man like this rides the clouds as his carriages and the sun and moon as his steeds. He wanders beyond the Four Seas; the alternations of life and death do not concern him, much less the notions of good and evil.

[*Chuang Tzu*, Chapter 2]

The fact is that these wanderings are journeys within ourselves, as is explained in a passage in the *Lieh Tzu*. Lieh Yü-k'ou in person—who presumably has not yet learned how to ride the wind—is being initiated by his master into the art of wandering:

Your concern is with traveling outwardly. You do not know how to go about inward contemplation. When traveling outwardly, we seek in things that which we lack; by means of inward contempla-tion, we find satisfaction within ourselves. This second way of traveling is the perfect one, the other is imperfect. . . . The perfect traveler does not know where he is going; the perfect contemplator does not know what he has before his eyes. [*Lieh Tzu*, Chapter 4]

These spiritual journeys are similar to journeys in dreams. We have seen that the Taoists considered dreaming to have just as much reality as waking. The *Lieh Tzu* tells how Huang Ti, the Yellow Emperor, realizing that his efforts to govern well were futile, went into retirement in order to discipline body and mind; he then had a dream, in which he wandered to the land of Hua-hsü, which "cannot be reached by boat, by carriage, or on foot, but only by a journey of the mind" (Chapter 2).

In the same work, we meet King Mu of Chou, who makes a fantastic dream-journey through the heavens, under the guidance of a magician; they reach a place where they can see neither sun nor moon above them, neither rivers nor seas beneath, but King Mu lacks sufficient virtue to face up to pure space without growing dizzy. He asks to go home, and immediately finds that he is back in his palace, where his courtiers believe him merely to have dozed off for a few minutes. The magician explains that all long journeys like this one take place only in the mind. King Mu, definitely inept when it came to wandering in the mind, thereupon set out on the famous travels that led him to the Queen Mother of the West, recounted in the earliest Chinese romance, the *Mu T'ien-tzu-chuan* (Son-of-Heaven Mu).

Wanderings of the soul are also a familiar theme in the literature of Ch'u as it has come down to us in the *Ch'u Tz'u*. This anthology contains, in particular, the poems of Ch'ü Yüan, the most famous of the ancient poets. In the *Li-*

sao the poet is ravished to heaven, where he visits marvelous places inhabited by characters out of mythology. But the best treatment of the theme is found in another poem, the *Yüan-yu* (Faraway Wandering), wrongly attributed to Ch'ü Yüan, but in fact dating from the first or second century B.C. Here the inspiration is exclusively Taoist: the poet, afflicted by the decadence of his times, vows to defy gravity, take flight heavenward, and wander far away. But how? While he is resting, troubled in his mind: "My spirit was suddenly ravished from my body, which was left by itself, looking like withered wood."

Later in the poem there is a reference to breathing methods, which must have been the essential feature of the technique for obtaining mystical flight, and which played an important role in later Taoism. We have already seen that Lao Tzu alludes to breathing exercises; Chuang Tzu says that the Perfect Men of ancient times "breathed deep breaths"—not merely from their throats and lungs like the mass of men, but from the whole body, starting with their heels. From this it is clear that these breathing methods were techniques for meditation similar to those that we will discuss in the next chapter, wholly inward exercises the aim of which was probably to concentrate the life forces and unify the powers of the mind.

Ecstasy freed the adept from all physical constraints, and he felt as if he were rising up and roaming beyond space and time, like the substanceless spirits dwelling in marvelous lands that Chuang Tzu talks about. His description of them ends with these words: "They protect all creatures from pestilence and ensure that the harvests are prosperous" (Chapter 1). The Taoist Holy Man believed that the greatest service he could render to the world was to withdraw from the world and devote himself to the pursuit of ecstasy.

MYSTICISM AND GOVERNMENT

One of the terms for the purification of the soul is *hsin chai*, which means, translated literally, "fasting of the heart." In classical religious practice, the *chai* was the ritual abstinence that preceded the sacrifices. Chuang Tzu refers to the *hsin chai* in a passage in which Confucius is supposed to be talking with his favorite disciple, Yen Hui (Chapter 4). Yen Hui is preparing for a visit to a tyrant, whom he hopes to civilize a little. Confucius, to whom Chuang Tzu once again lends Taoist ideas, warns him against aggressiveness, which would be sure to awaken a dangerous response in his redoubtable adversary. He advises him before leaving to purify himself and concentrate his mind by fasting (*chai*), and then explains what he means:

"Unify your will. Don't listen with your ears, listen with your heart [mind]; then don't listen with your heart, listen with your [soul-] breath. For hearing is limited by the ears, the heart is limited by its being adapted to particular objects, but the breath is a passive vacuity. The Tao dwells where there is the void, and the void is obtained by the fasting of the heart."

After he had experienced the fasting of the heart Yen Hui felt as if he had lost his individuality:

"Before I was able to use this method, I was aware of my self; now that I have been able to use it, it's as if I, Hui, had never existed. Is this the void?"

"Exactly so," replied Confucius. [Chapter 4]

We are here in the presence of a particular feature of

Taoist mysticism: its practical efficacy. Psychic purification is a method for living in one's time and for "acting without acting." Totally inhabited by the Tao, the Holy Man possesses a form of Te (mystical power) that exerts a beneficent, but imperceptible, influence on others. The Taoists strongly emphasize the need for what we would call "hiding one's light under a bushel." The spiritual light must never be externalized, for it might dazzle people and cease being beneficent. The Holy Man's power is immense, provided it is kept secret.

Even in everyday life, contacts with others are dangerous unless both parties are utterly disinterested. Animals are never deceived about this; they intuitively sense the oncomer's state of mind:

> A young man who lived near the seashore was very fond of seagulls. Every morning, he went down to the beach to play with them, and the gulls arrived by hundreds without hesitation. One day, the young man's father said to him: "I've heard that the seagulls play familiarly with you. Catch me a few so that I can play with them as well."
>
> Next morning, the young man went down to the beach, but the gulls played in the air above his head, and not one came down to him. [*Lieh Tzu*, Chapter 2]

This explains why Yen Hui had to empty his heart before approaching the tyrant.

The same thing holds for ruling a state. All the Chinese philosophers were preoccupied with the problem of government. For all his individualism, Chuang Tzu is no exception. Living, as he did, in particularly troubled times, he could not help having ideas of his own on the problems of war and peace, order and disorder. But what he says about them is as unrealistic as anything could be. He naturally condemns war, not because we must love our neighbor (which, from Chuang Tzu's point of view, is the best way to harm him), but because worldly action is always futile. All a ruler needs to do to rule, he proclaims, is look after his soul. In Chapter 25 he tells of a king of Wei who wonders whether to make war on Ch'i. The king's minister and his general have opposite views in the matter, and start calling each other scoundrels. The Taoist Hua Tzu steps in and says: "The one who is so good at preaching war against Ch'i is undeniably a scoundrel, but the one who is so good at saying the opposite is another scoundrel. And anyone who calls the partisans of war and their opponents scoundrels is also a scoundrel." "What must I do, then?" the king asks. "Sire, seek the Tao, that is all you need do."

Convinced that true power comes from the presence of the Tao and from nothing else, Chuang Tzu urges the leader of men to cultivate holiness. A king, responsible for natural order, ought to be like the Immortals in their paradises, who ensure good harvests. The mere presence of a Holy Man is enough to bring prosperity to a whole region. So the king (later, the emperor) is asked to live as an ascetic and to refrain from interfering. Philanthropic zeal, missionizing, and lawmaking are sins against Heaven or against nature. The ancient missionizing kings, whom the Confucianists valued so highly, merely succeeded in perverting people; they destroyed the natural spontaneity that all creatures once had. The first inventors were no better:

When horses lived free on the prairies, they ate grass and drank water. When they were pleased, they rubbed their necks together; when they were angry, they turned back to back and kicked up their heels at each other. This was all they knew. But once they were bridled and bitted and harnessed, they learned how to be vicious, how to get their head and bolt, trying to get rid of the bit and the bridle. [Chapter 9]

In the days before men were perverted

they stayed at home without knowing how to do the least thing, they strolled around without knowing where they were going. They stuffed themselves with food, slapped each other on the back, and lived free and easy. They had no talent for anything else. But when the [Confucianist] sages appeared with their ritual kowtowing and their music, presuming to discipline people's behavior throughout the world, when they started flaunting their virtue in the hope of conquering people's minds, men began scrambling after knowledge and arguing over wealth; it was no longer possible to stop them. This was the error of these sages. [Chapter 9]

Probably taking over an old myth, Chuang Tzu tells the following fable as an illustration of the damage that can be done by imprudent civilizers:

The ruler of the Southern Ocean was Shu; the ruler of the Northern Ocean was Hu. The ruler of the central region was Chaos. Shu and Hu sometimes met in the territory of Chaos, who treated them very courteously. They discussed how they could best repay his kindness. "Everyone has seven openings for seeing, hearing, eating, and breathing. Chaos doesn't have any. Let's try boring some into him!" So they undertook to bore one hole into him each day. On the seventh day Chaos died. [Chapter 7]

Chaos had the perfection of a sphere; it possessed the original simplicity (*p'u*) of an undifferentiated being, the autonomy of the embryo, which is a concentration of life folded in upon itself. An untimely zeal would wish to make it like everybody else, and initiate it into civilized life by giving it the sense organs that destroy its unity. The myth is a perfect symbol of the Founding Kings' original sin.

Chuang Tzu is fond of setting what pertains to Heaven

in opposition to what pertains to man, or in other words, what pertains to nature and what to society. According to him, we must discard all artifice, even the techniques that seem to lighten our tasks, but in fact quickly sap our morals. The Taoist chooses to live obscurely, in tiny communities such as were imagined to have existed in an age of perfect virtue. The states were small, with few inhabitants; the people used knotted cords instead of writing. They were contented with what food and clothing they had, took pleasure in their own customs, and felt at home. Neighboring districts were within sight of each other, and the crowing cocks and barking dogs of one could be heard in the other; yet the people grew old and died without ever having dealings with their neighbors. In those days government was indeed perfect (*Chuang Tzu*, Chapter 10; *Lao Tzu*, Chapter 80).

IN PRAISE OF INUTILITY

The Taoist Holy Man puts himself at "the center of the ring" and lets things happen spontaneously. Hence he deliberately does nothing to promote the good of the community: holiness and profane utility are incompatible. Like his predecessor, Lao Tzu, who affirms that all power to produce an effect lies in the Void and that we must be without merit, Chuang Tzu proclaims the superior value of uselessness. A tree's chances of growing tall and venerable depend on its wood being worthless to the carpenter.

At Ching-shih in Sung, the ground is eminently suitable for growing catalpas, cypresses, and mulberries. As soon as the tree trunks reach one or two arm-lengths around, they are cut down by people wanting monkey poles; those that measure three or four spans are cut down to make fine beams for houses; and those that measure seven or eight spans are cut down to make coffins for the families of noblemen and rich merchants. Thus, instead of lasting their natural lifetime, they come to a premature end at the woodsman's axe when half grown: this is the misfortune caused them by the good quality of their wood. Similarly, when victims are offered to the river to appease it, an ox with a white forehead, a pig with a turned-up snout, or a girl with piles is not suitable: this is what the sorcerers and priests say, and these signs are considered inauspicious. But the Sage takes them to represent good luck.

. . .

The mountain, owing to its forests, itself attracts the rascals that will deprive it of them; tallow, because it can burst into flame, destroys itself; it is because it is edible that the cassia is cut down; it is because its sap is useful that the lacquer tree is bled. All men know the advantage of being useful, but they do not know the advantage of being useless. [Chapter 4]

But, of course, useful and useless belong to the class of complementary notions that the Taoists reject. Moreover, it is a constant fact that simply being useless is not enough to keep you out of danger. Uselessness in the Taoist sense has its bearing on the absolute:

Chuang Tzu was traveling over a mountain when he saw a huge tree with splendid foliage. Some woodsmen who were there seemed to disdain it. He asked them why. "It's no good for anything," came the reply.

Thereupon Chuang Tzu said: "This tree, because its wood is good for nothing, will die a natural death."

When he had left the mountain, the master stopped by at an old friend's. The friend was delighted to see him, and ordered a servant to kill a goose and cook it. The servant asked: "Which shall I kill? The one that can cackle or the one that can't?"

"Kill the one that can't cackle," said the host.

The next day, the disciples asked Chuang Tzu: "That tree we saw on the mountain yesterday, because it is good for nothing, will die a natural death. And today, this goose of our host's—because it was of no use, it lost its life. Which position would you choose?"

Chuang Tzu replied laughingly: "If I chose a position halfway between being useful and being useless, I would seem to be right; but this would not really be the case, and I would certainly get into trouble. Whereas things are different for the wanderer, borne along by the Tao and Te: he knows neither praise nor blame. Now a dragon, now a serpent, he changes with the change of time and does not consent to specialization; now he rises, now he falls, adapting himself to the rhythm of nature. He takes his ease at the origin of all things. Things are things for him, and he is not a thing for things, so how could he get into trouble? Such was the method of Huang Ti and Shen Nung. But this was not the case for the passions inherent in the Ten Thousand Creatures and for common morality. For every union is destined to be separated, every achievement to be destroyed, every corner to be flattened, every eminence to be overthrown, and every activity is destined to failure. Talent breeds jealousy, lack of intelligence breeds deceit. None of these situations is preferable to another. Ah! Think on all this, my disciples. May the Tao and Te be your only refuge." [Chapter 20]

INFLUENCES OF PHILOSOPHICAL TAOISM

Emperor Chen-tsung of the Sung (A.D. 998–1022), a practicing Taoist, once invited his closest ministers to a banquet. When the talk turned to Chuang Tzu, he sent for the chapter called "Autumn Floods," and a maiden in green was asked to read the text aloud. Everyone stood up and listened to it reverentially.

The reason Chen-tsung chose a maiden to read "Autumn Floods," one of the most philosophical and literary chapters in the whole *Chuang Tzu* is that, in the Far East, virgins are considered to have exceptionally pure voices. Such a voice was essential to bring out the poetical beauty of the text.*

* The maiden in green probably symbolized Spring also, in order to invoke the powers of Autumn referred to at the beginning of the chapter in question.

The literary importance of the *Chuang Tzu* has always been recognized. Even before Ssu-ma Ch'ien expressed his admiration, the author of the T'ien-hsia chapter made much of Chuang Chou's merits as a stylist; he even seems somewhat taken aback by a freedom in the expression that must have been rare in the prose authors. He admits that he cannot make head nor tail of most of it, but he does sense that the oddness and eccentricity of the style were a means for this independence-loving genius to express the theme of mystical evasion: "Though his writings are grandiose, they are tolerant and never hurt anybody. His style, full of variety and unexpected turns of phrase, is admirable. The richness of his work is inexhaustible: above, he roams with the Creator of all creatures; below, he is the friend of those who know how to expel life and death from their awareness and know neither beginning nor end." Whether Chuang Tzu's satire never hurt anybody is debatable, but a capacity for universal sympathy is perceptible behind many of the anecdotes in which he appears. Because the universe is one, a close communion with all creatures is possible provided we are disinterested; and since nature is an immense phantasmagoria, it is best expressed through fantasy. This is what Chuang Tzu does in his wholly poetical manner of philosophizing. To a lesser extent, Lao Tzu, Lieh Tzu, and Huai-nan Tzu do the same. The writers of the Taoist school have a style of their own: they all make use of myth and legend, and their rhythmical prose frequently attains heights of incantatory grandeur.

Their influence on arts and letters was enormous. No one can understand Chinese poetry without having assimilated the thought of the Taoist philosophers and the themes developed later by Neo-Taoism. Taoist influence on monochrome landscape painting was, of course, considerable, either directly so, or coming in via the Taoist-influenced Buddhist sect, Ch'an (Zen). On a less obvious level, the same mysticism is the inspiration behind the paintings of bamboos, reeds, and rocks that compose the subtle genre greatly prized by connoisseurs. In the different arts cultivated by the educated classes (besides painting, we should add calligraphy and music), the influence of Taoism and Ch'an was fundamental; it was their influence that made this artistic activity more than just distraction or snobbery and gave it a genuinely spiritual dimension. On the other hand, Taoist sculpture, mediocre in quality and extremely rare (except in the popular genres), cannot bear comparison with Buddhist sculpture, the prodigious richness of which is well known.

THE TAOIST RELIGION

At first sight, philosophical Taoism and magico-religious Taoism appear to have little in common. There are worlds between the thought of Lao Tzu and Chuang Tzu and what Chavannes has called the "hodgepodge of coarse-grained superstitions" that sprang up in the second century A.D., and indeed all the historians distinguish between the philosophical school of the Tao (*tao chia*) and the Taoist religion (*tao chiao*).

The differences between the two are manifest indeed, and there can be no denying they exist. But it is no less certain that the mystical tradition of the philosophers was carried over into what is sometimes called Neo-Taoism. This movement claims a large measure of kinship with the doctrine of Lao Tzu and the *tao chia*. However, this original philosophical stock was profoundly transformed by graftings of different religious and magical traditions: some were indigenous (all kinds of popular beliefs and techniques), others foreign. The most important of the alien traditions was Buddhism, which gradually won currency and support from the first century A.D. on.

This syncretism has produced an enormous mass of scriptures found in the collection of patristic writings called the *Tao Tsang* (Taoist Canon), drawn up on the lines of the *San Tsang* (the Buddhist Tripitaka) and containing no less than 1,464 titles. This canon has gone through many vicissitudes in the course of its history, yet it shows up as a well-organized whole. The scriptures are divided into three main sections (plus four appendixes): these three sections are called *tung*, a word whose root meaning is "cave," but which also means "to communicate," "to see through the mysteries." The main texts were obtained by revelation: they are a means of communication between the gods and men, by which men can see through the mysteries and enter into supernatural life. Further, certain sacred texts were said to have been hidden in mountain caverns. This explains why the *Tao Tsang* is split up into *tung*, a term that evokes both mysterious caverns and dealings with the sacred powers.

Behind each *tung* there is an original text revealed by one of the three divinities that head the vast Taoist pantheon. The first section (*tung chen*) is thus placed under the patronage of Yüan Shih T'ien Tsun (the Heavenly Elder of the Primal Origin), the supreme divinity, a direct emanation of the Tao; the second section is dedicated to T'ai Shang Tao Chün (the Very Noble Lord of the Tao); and the third to T'ai Shang Lao Chün (the Very Noble Lord Lao, who is none other than Lao Tzu deified. But according to another, slightly different, theory the three *tung* are presided over by three lords representing three persons of Yüan Shih T'ien Tsun.

Hence we have a triad in which, it will be noticed, Lao Tzu takes merely third place; he is said to be the disciple of Tao Chün, himself the disciple of T'ien Tsun. But since the theories held by the various sects never ranked as compulsory dogma, they did not prevent people under the T'ang from considering T'ai Shang Lao Chün, i.e. Lao Tzu, to be the sole revealer of the main texts in all three sections.

LAO TZU DEIFIED

If Lao Tzu, deified as Laσ Chün, does not always appear to be the most important member of the Taoist pantheon, his deification is nevertheless of very ancient date. We have already seen that in the second century B.C., at the time when Ssu-ma Ch'ien was writing the *Historical Memoirs*, Lao Tzu was already a legendary figure credited by some with fabled longevity. Under the second Han he became a veritable god. In an inscription composed in A.D. 165 on the occasion of a sacrifice held in Po Chou Temple on the orders of Emperor Huan, it is stated that for some followers of the Tao, Lao Tzu is an emanation of primordial chaos and is coeternal with the Three Luminaries (Sun, Moon, and Stars). He is even compared to P'an Ku, the mythological First Man. When P'an Ku died, "his head became the Four Peaks, his eyes became the sun and moon." Similarly, when Lao Tzu died, he "changed his body," and (the quotation is taken not from the inscription but from a more explicit later text)

his left eye became the sun, his right the moon; his head became the Kunlun Mountains; his beard became the planets and mansions; his bones became the dragons; his flesh became the four-footed animals; his intestines became the serpents; his belly became the sea; his fingers became the Five Peaks; his body hair became the trees and grasses; his heart became the [constellation] Flowery Canopy; and his two kidneys joined together to become the Father and Mother of the Real [*chen-yao fu mu*].*

The inscription also attributes to Lao Tzu, like the Buddha, a series of human avatars. These are believed to be the

---

* Chen Luan, *Hsiao-tao Lun* (Treatise Deriding the Tao), quoted in Henri Maspero, "Le Taoïsme," Vol. 2 of *Mélanges posthumes sur les religions et l'histoire de la Chine* (Paris, 1950), p. 108.

different personalities he adopts when coming down to earth "to instruct the ancient rulers," the holy founders of civilization.

The same Emperor Huan raised altars to Huang Ti, Lao Tzu, and surprisingly enough, to the Buddha. Worship of the Buddha must already have been very widespread for him to be officially adopted in this way. But in point of fact Buddhism was very poorly understood in those days; people made few distinctions between it and Taoism, from which the first translators of sūtras were obliged to borrow their philosophical and religious terminology. The Buddha was thought to be none other than Lao Tzu himself, who had departed toward the West. Some time later, the Taoists exploited this legend to combat Buddhist propaganda, and fabricated a famous apocryphal work—the *Lao Tzu Hua-hu Ching* (The Book of Lao Tzu's Conversions of the Barbarians). For centuries this book was a point of contention between Taoists and Buddhists; often condemned by the imperial authorities, it continued to circulate nonetheless until the thirteenth century, undergoing various modifications and additions, and even being illustrated. One of these versions deals with the 81 avatars of Lao Tzu's conversions. In one he is the Buddha Sakyamuni; in the last, he is Mani, the founder of Manichaeanism.

The inscription of A.D. 165 also alludes, rather cryptically, to meditational and long-life practices supposed to have been known and, presumably, taught by Lao Tzu. In a hagiographical anthology dating from virtually the same period, it is again said that Lao Tzu and his disciple, the Master of the Pass, were proficient in this kind of exercise. There are also references to the journey to the West and the conversion of the barbarians:

Lao Tzu ... knew how to nourish his vital energy; he valued the art of acquiring it and not expending it. ... He lived for more than 80 years: the *Shih Chi* says more than 200 years. In those days he was called the Hidden Sage. ... Later on, as the virtue of the Chou declined, Lao Tzu climbed into a carriage drawn by a green ox and entered the land of Ta Ch'in [the eastern provinces of the Roman Empire]. [*Lieh-hsien Chuan, IX*]

The Keeper of the Pass, Yin Hsi, ... was versed in the esoteric sciences and always fed on the purest essences. He kept his virtue secret and went prudently about his business so that no one in his day ever noticed him. When Lao Tzu departed toward the West, Yin Hsi, who had already perceived his emanation, knew that a sage was going to pass through. He observed the colors of the signs that preceded him and waited for him on the way; he actually found Lao Tzu. Lao Tzu knew for his part that Yin Hsi was an extraordinary person; he wrote a book for him and gave it to him. Then they departed together beyond the Moving Sands and converted the barbarians. They fed on sesame seeds. No one knows what finally became of them. [*Lieh-hsien Chuan, X*]

Hence, as early as the second Han, Lao Tzu was presented as an adept of the long-life practices that were to characterize him in most later Taoist sects. As we shall see, increasing one's vital energy or avoiding its expenditure was the fundamental principle of the Taoist sexual and respiratory theories; feeding on unusual substances made it possible to avoid consuming cereals (*pi ku*), a form of abstinence that actually implied the rejection of all vulgar foodstuffs. Here Lao Tzu and the Master of the Pass, wandering through the Western lands, find sesame—not a Chinese plant, but one held to have health-giving virtues.

Hence we can legitimately suppose that people paid particular attention in those days to the passages in the *Tao Te Ching* alluding more or less clearly to the "nurture of the life principle," and that other passages were improperly interpreted to mean the same thing. The commentary of Ho Shang Kung is significant in this respect: in the eyes of its author, the *Tao Te Ching* deals both with the cultivation of the life principles and with the art of government by means of *wu-wei*. In this way, Lao Tzu became an exceptionally important figure, and because the *Tao Te Ching* became recognized as the fundamental book of the Taoist school, the various branches of Taoism came together to form a single movement. Another result was that after sharing the primacy of the "Huang-Lao" doctrine with Huang Ti, Lao Tzu finally won the day by becoming Lao Chün, the revealer of sacred texts and the savior of mankind. However, Huang Ti, to whom mythology ascribed a number of inventions, and who seems to have been worshipped by the guilds of metalworkers and other technicians from a very early date, took on the specialized role of patron of occult sciences and medicine. (Medicine subsequently broke with Taoism as it had already broken with magic.)

It was under the T'ang dynasty that Lao Tzu received more official honors than at any other moment in history. The emperors of this house had the same family name, Li, as the author of the *Tao Te Ching*. In A.D. 667, Kao Tsung gave him the title T'ai-shang Hsüan-yüan Huang-ti (Very Noble Celestial and Primordial Emperor) and, in 737, an official course of study in Taoist philosophy was established, something never before done. There were even examinations dealing with the Taoist classics, which for a time became as important as the Confucian *ching*. As many as 1,687 Taoist monasteries were then in existence, and royal princesses are known to have become nuns.

Nonetheless, Lao Tzu's predominance was far from being acknowledged by all Taoists. Not only was Lao Chün often held to be subordinate to Yüan Shih T'ien Tsun, but also certain authors even contested his divine nature. To Ko Hung,* Lao Tzu was a man of exceptional gifts but not a divinity; he concedes that Lao Tzu wrote treatises on long life in addition to the *Tao Te Ching*. Nevertheless, he adds that Lao Tzu was in favor of apathy and had no desires, long life being his only aim.

As we have seen, opinions about Lao Tzu differed according to milieu and period: for some, he was the supreme divinity, the personification of the Tao; for others, he was merely an emanation of Yüan Shih T'ien Tsun, or his disciple; and for still others, he was merely a great sage to whom men ascribed very diverse opinions.

CHANG TAO-LING AND THE HEAVENLY MASTERS

If Lao Tzu is mainly thought of as the patron of the *tao chia*, the personage often regarded as the founder of the Taoist religion is someone quite different: Chang Ling (or Chang Tao-ling), who is said to have been born during the reign of Emperor Huan (A.D. 147–67). He learned the methods for achieving long life and concocted the elixir of immortality; then he went into Szechwan province, where he wrote books and did missionary work with great popular success. Converts to his Tao made a contribution of five bushels of rice, hence the name Five Bushel Sect; it was also called the Heavenly Masters Sect, after the titles borne by the leaders of Chang Tao-ling's movement. The movement spread rapidly; taking advantage of the decline of the Han

---

* One of the most important Taoist authors. He wrote the *Pao P'u Tzu*, a work containing numerous references to alchemy, and the *Shen-hsien Chuan*, a collection of lives of Taoists.

dynasty, the founder's son, followed by his grandson, organized an independent state in Hanchung. Meanwhile in eastern China another movement, called the Yellow Turbans, almost overthrew the dynasty in A.D. 184 by rousing the people of eight provinces to revolt. The Yellow Turbans, whose doctrine was known as the Great Peace Tao or Great Justice Tao (T'ai P'ing Tao), proclaimed the imminent advent of a new era and promised the founding of a utopian order similar to that described in a book of revelations, the *T'ai P'ing Ching*.

Even though these two movements seem to have been mutually independent and were geographically far apart, they do have numerous common features. Their leaders set themselves up as healers, which must have been one reason why they were so successful. To heal the sick they made much use of talismans and lustral water, but since sickness was to them a sign of sin, their main healing technique was confession and penitence; the sick were sent into retreat to reflect upon their sins. These religious and military leaders also proved capable of organizing the territory under their control; the faithful masses were split up into kinds of parishes under the authority of a hierarchy of priest-magicians. In the Five Bushel Sect, the supreme leader was the Heavenly Master; lower down, the faithful obtained ranks and titles according to the stages they had reached in religious observance.

With the Five Bushel Sect and the T'ai P'ing Tao, we are in the presence of a collective Taoism far different from that of the small philosophical groups comprising a few disciples gathered around a master. For even though the Yellow Turbans were finally annihilated by the Han armies, the Heavenly Masters Sect lived on and spread throughout the land. A kind of hereditary patriarchate was even set up, and has continued down to modern times.

Taoism changed as a result; it became infused with moral considerations, particularly under the influence of Buddhism. Religious observance included large-scale festivals during which, at the equinoxes, offerings were made to gods who had nothing specifically Taoist about them. At the solstices, the members of the sect made sacrifices to the dead, as all the Chinese did; but beforehand they received healing charms and amulets supposed to repel demons. Some of these festivals were orgiastic in nature and were finally eliminated; but other festivals of a more sober kind, are found in other sects also, all making great use of talismans. However, alongside this collective Taoism, there was always an individual, esoteric Taoism; adherents often practiced both at once.

A remarkable thing is that, from the very start of the movement, the Heavenly Masters used the *Tao Te Ching* in their religious teaching. They even fixed its length at 5000 characters and wrote a commentary* to instruct fresh converts. As was to be expected, they interpreted Lao Tzu's thought in a way that strayed much further from the original meaning than Ho Shang Kung's commentary ever did. For instance, the beginning of Chapter 10 ("Let your physical soul and your spiritual soul embrace the Unity") is glossed as follows:

P'o (physical or seminal soul) comes from *po* (white). This is why the Essence is white, the same color as the Primordial Breath. The body is the carriage of the Essence; the Essence tends to fall, and that is why it has to be protected on its journey. . . . The One

---

* A large fragment of this "lost" commentary, called the *Hsiang Erh*, has recently been discovered and published.

is the Tao. Yet where can it be found in the body of man? And what is meant by "protecting it"? The One does not dwell in the body of man. If something comes and takes possession of the body, that is always due to one of the vulgar deceiving forms of magic current in the world; it is not the true Tao. The One is outside Heaven and Earth, but it comes in between Heaven and Earth. It never stops coming and going in the human body; hence it is everywhere inside the skin and not in one particular spot. The One, when it is dispersed, is the Breath; when it is gathered together, it is T'ai Shang Lao Chün. Its home is the Kunlun. Whether we say the Void or Natural Spontaneity or the Nameless, it is always the same Unity. Now, he [Lao Chün] promulgates the commandments of the Tao and teaches men that they must observe them scrupulously; this is what is meant by "protecting the One." If a man does not behave in conformity with these precepts, he loses the One. The vulgar deceiving forms of magic give names to the One according to the vital organ where it is supposed to dwell; they want men to close their eyes when meditating and wish to obtain happiness in this way. This is wrong, for by so doing we put a distance between ourselves and life.

Sin is not what pleases the Tao; we must therefore purify ourselves of all sin and be faultless in our behavior. [*Hsiang Erh*]

It will be seen that this commentary opposes the true Tao to the false doctrines. The true Tao is, of course, the doctrine of the sect; the false doctrines are all the other religious or magical movements, the Taoist movements included. The *Hsiang Erh* commentary and the *T'ai P'ing Ching* often mention the commandments of the Tao, which are revealed, for they emanate directly from Heaven. The main precept concerns the duty of filial piety, which is also one of the main Confucian virtues and can be said to have been the foundation of Chinese ethics for all time. In fact, once Taoism became a popular militant religion, it was inevitably led to give greater importance to moral considerations. The most esoteric and individualistic Taoism of all—that of the alchemists—itself attached great significance to the observance of the virtues, which was considered a prerequisite for their work.

THE IMMORTALS (HSIEN-JEN, SHEN-HSIEN)

Though their methods differed, all the small Taoist sects were after the same thing: immortality. This was not the wholly spiritual immortality sought by Chuang Tzu, but actual physical immortality. Adepts could choose among several methods that were supposed to restore to the body the pure energies it possessed at its birth, in accordance with the precept of Lao Tzu, who had so much admiration for the vigor of the infant. They were certain to live for a thousand years and then, weary of the world after such a long time, to be able to leave it, and rising up toward the heavens, "ride the white clouds and reach the home of the gods" (*Chuang Tzu*).

"Ascended to Heaven at the height of the day" was henceforth to be the stock formula to describe the final apotheosis of a Taoist who had succeeded in transubstantiating his physical being. True, some departed more discreetly; they seemed to die like ordinary mortals, but their death was merely apparent, for if the coffin was opened after a lapse of time, the body had disappeared and been replaced by the dead man's staff, sword, or sandals.

Where do the Immortals go? Some go to heaven. Or to *a* heaven, if we are to be accurate, for a number of Taoist heavens have come to be invented, more like complicated city halls than paradises. More poetical are the marvelous isles (already referred to by Chuang Tzu and Lieh Tzu) that stand in the eastern sea; or the Kunlun Mountains, which rise far away in the west of China.

According to Lieh Tzu the supernatural islands were

formerly five in number; they were 7000 *li* apart, but their inhabitants, who were all Immortals, considered themselves neighbors and flew around paying each other visits. But the islands were borne on the backs of giant turtles. Along came a giant, who used a fishing line to hook the turtles that held up two of the islands, and then there were three: Fang-hu, Ying-chou, and P'eng-lai. Ssu-ma Ch'ien says:

> During the reigns of Kings Wei [357–20 B.C.] and Hsüan [319–301 B.C.] of Ch'i and King Chao of Yen [311–279 B.C.], the practice began of sending men out to sea in search of the three sacred mountains, . . . reportedly not very far away from men. Unfortunately, just as the men are about to reach the shores, the boats are swept back and away by the wind. In earlier times, some people actually managed to reach them: there, the Blessed and the drug that prevents death can be found; there, all things, birds, and four-footed animals are white, and the palaces are made of gold and silver. When these people were just short of the mountains, they could see them from afar like a cloud. When they arrived, the three sacred mountains were washed away by the waves. . . . In short, no one has ever been able to land there. There is not one of the rulers who would not like to have gone there.

According to the historian, these legends were told by the magicians who lived in the coast provinces of Yen and Ch'i. They encouraged Ch'in Shih Huang Ti and Emperor Wu of the Han to send out sea expeditions with orders to make contact with the Immortals and lay hands on the elixir, but they failed. One of Ch'in Shih Huang Ti's expeditions is supposed to have achieved the colonization of a "quiet, fertile spot" that may have been Japan.

As for the Kunlun Mountains, they comprised three or nine tiers, which means that the person who scaled them could reach Heaven. There were the same number of terraces going downwards, and thus the subterranean waters, the abode of the dead, were united with the home of the gods. During his grand tour of the West in his eight-horsed chariot, Son-of-Heaven Mu visited the Kunlun, which he scaled "in order to gaze upon the palace of Huang Ti, and he raised a cairn to commemorate his visit. Then he was the guest of the Queen Mother of the West (Hsi Wang Mu), who offered him a banquet on the banks of Jasper Lake. And the Queen sang for the King, while he accompanied her, but the words of her song were sad" (*Lieh Tzu*, Chapter 3).

Hsi Wang Mu is an important figure in Taoist mythology and folklore. She seems to have started out in life as a mountain spirit whose appearance, if we are to believe the *Shan Hai Ching* (Book of Mountains and Seas), was none too prepossessing: she had human form, but the tail of a leopard and the teeth of a tiger. Later, however, she became a divinity with rather more charm, and the Taoists took her for the Fairy Queen of the Immortals. A Taoist romance tells how Hsi Wang Mu came to visit Emperor Wu of the Han; she offered him some marvelous peaches, and revealed certain things that he was never capable of turning to his profit.

The artists of the Han were fond of depicting the Immortals on miscellaneous objects—lacquer boxes, bronze mirrors—or on the painted or sculptured walls of temples or tombs. They generally depicted them with wings or covered all over with feathers. The bronze mirrors decorated with Taoist spirits were usually accompanied by an inscription such as this: "The Imperial Workshop has made this mirror, a true masterpiece; on it you can see an Immortal, who knows nothing of old age. When he is thirsty, he drinks at the Jade Springs; when he is hungry, he eats marvelous jujubes. He wanders freely through the world, and takes his ease in the far-flung regions of the universe."

Some of the *hsien-jen* are depicted with a kind of lump on their heads; sometimes the heads are swollen out of all proportion, and this peculiarity is also found at a much later date in the representations of the God of Long Life, Shou-hsing, one of the most familiar figures in the popular pantheon. This cranial hypertrophy is not due to water on the brain; neither is it the sign of prodigious intelligence. It signifies that these Blessed Beings have proved capable of fortifying their brains (not thought organs, but reservoirs of vital energy) by the appropriate methods, just as the bat does. This animal, a frequent feature in Chinese decoration, is one of the symbols of long life because it was held to live an exceptionally long time owing to its frequenting caves, where it was believed to feed on concretions with marvelous life-giving qualities.

The conception of the Bird-Immortals has links with a very ancient belief concerning the inhabitants of the eastern regions of China (modern Hopei and Shantung) in the days when these regions were still barbaric. These coastlands were inhabited by birdmen, whose appearance must have been similar to that of the *hsien-jen*. This explains why the magicians' propaganda at the close of the Warring States period, and under the Ch'in and the Han—propaganda that made much of the Isles of the Blessed and the way to immortality—originated in the same regions, which have often stood out as centers of intense religious activity.

Some of the Bird-barbarians looked like herons or cranes. They performed ritual dances: the dance of the pheasants, which invoked thunder, and the dance of the cranes, which was doubtless a stilt dance like those still extant both in

Taoism and in folklore. The crane is the Taoist Immortals'
bird *par excellence*. It was believed to live for more than a
thousand years and to be capable of breathing with its neck
bent, a technique for making the breath supple that is imi-
tated by the Taoists. The immaculate whiteness of its plum-
age was naturally a symbol of purity, but its cinnabar-
colored head shows that, like the bat, it knows how to
preserve its life potency, and that inwardly it is pure Yang
and has no Yin, the death principle. Hence the crane is the
Immortal's mount when he frolics in the skies.

LONG-LIFE PRACTICES

Since Lao Tzu was supposed to have been a master of
long-life practices and magic, Ko Hung, a convinced expert
on the subject, thought much more of him than of Chuang
Tzu, who is severely condemned in the *Pao P'u Tzu* for not
stressing life more than death and for rejecting the physical
methods. However, Chuang Tzu did not reject all these
methods; he seems to have recognized at least some disciplining of the breath. Though it is hard to know how far he
took this, his disciples seem to have interpreted his mysticism as one of the means for obtaining great longevity. For
instance, in one of the comparatively late chapters of the
Chuang Tzu (Chapter 11), we find the famous story about
Kuang Ch'eng Tzu, Huang Ti's master, who gave the following advice to his pupil:

Hold your vital spirits in the embrace of perfect quietness, and your
body will be governed of itself. Be quiet, be pure; neither weary
your body nor disturb your vital essence, and then you will live a
long time. Let your eyes have nothing to see, your ears nothing to
hear, your heart nothing to know; then your spirits will preserve the

integrity of your body and it will remain alive for a long time. Watch over what is within you, and close off that which is without; for too much learning is a curse. I will lead you to the summit of the Great Light, to the source of the Yang-in-its-perfection; I will lead you to the Gates of Darkness, to the source of the Yin-without-admixture.

The idea that absolute tranquillity makes it possible to increase inner potency and longevity by preventing expenditures of energy caused by the desire to act is here put forward in a particularly vigorous manner. It explains why the ideal ruler had to practice *wu-wei*. The ancient sovereigns wore headdresses consisting of a fringe of pearls to cover their eyes and flaps to stop their ears. In this way they avoided the expenditures of vitality involved in the use of the senses. Because some sense organs are openings through which the vital souls or spirits are tempted to escape, they have to be watched and the spirits have to be kept in their respective places: this, essentially, is the aim of Taoist hygiene. But the procedures by which this plenitude of energy may be acquired are numerous, ranging from the absolute tranquillity preached by the successors of the philosophers down to the assorted formulas of Neo-Taoism. The former was for a time overshadowed by the latter, without ever disappearing completely; but it reappeared around the T'ang period in a new form called internal alchemy or embryonic respiration.

In order to understand these different internal and external methods, we need to keep in mind the idea that people then had of the human body. It was thought to be an exact replica of the cosmos, each of its different features having a correspondence with something in the external world. The seen world is an emanation of the Tao. At first, the Yin and the Yang were joined together within the Tao, forming an undifferentiated breath called the Primordial Breath (*yüan-ch'i*). When the Yin and the Yang separated, they formed Heaven and Earth, and the mixture of the two gave birth to men and all creatures. Hence we are made up of Yin and Yang, which are heavenly and earthly "breaths." In particular, our higher soul, *hun*, is heavenly, and the lower soul, *p'o*, is earthly. Further, the cosmos is formed of five space-time sectors (the four cardinal points corresponding to the four seasons, and the center). These five sectors (symbolized by colors) correspond, on earth, to the Five Elements and the Five Sacred Peaks and, in man, to the Five Viscera. Each viscus is nourished by its corresponding element at the appropriate season. All this results in a kind of code that makes it possible to adapt the life of the microcosm to that of the macrocosm. The aim was to choose from the external world those substances that were the most appropriate for nourishing the viscera; in addition, it was necessary to ensure a proper circulation of the life principles inside the body by avoiding obstructions, the main causes of illness. These correspondences may be summarized as follows:

Elements	*Colors*	*Directions*	*Seasons*	*Viscera*	*Savors*
WOOD	Green	East	Spring	Liver	Acid
FIRE	Red	South	Summer	Heart	Bitter
EARTH	Yellow	Center	———	Spleen	Sweet
METAL	White	West	Autumn	Lungs	Acrid
WATER	Black	North	Winter	Kidneys	Salt

To a great extent, the Taoists shared the preoccupations of the physicians, and many healers can be found among their ranks. But their ambitions went further and their methods were different. The body was supposed to be made up of three sections called the three Fields of Cinnabar. (As we will see, cinnabar was the basic ingredient of the elixir of immortality.) The Higher Field of Cinnabar is in the brain; the second is near the heart; the third is underneath the navel, and near it there is the Sea of the Breath (*ch'i-hai*). The Fields of Cinnabar, like all the regions of the body, are the homes of guardian spirits (*shen*); but they are also inhabited by maleficent creatures, the Three Worms or the three cadaveric demons, which attack their host's vitality, each in its own way. The higher demon attacks the eyes and causes other ills in the head; the middle demon strikes at the belly and the guts; the lower demon causes kidney ailments, drains a man of his essence and marrow, withers his bones, and makes his blood anemic. Furthermore, the worms have an interest in seeing that the person who houses them dies as fast as possible, for his death sets them free. This is why they encourage him to do evil deeds, and periodically go off and tell on him to the heavenly judges, who promptly reduce his allotted lifespan. So adepts have to rid themselves of these three demons; in order to do so, they have to give up all ordinary foodstuffs, the essence of which keeps the Three Worms alive. They must abstain from consuming meat, wine, and strong-smelling plants, as well as cereals. Instead of these, they must live off substances capable of killing the three demons: above all, herbs, but also mineral substances.

The internal demons have to be expelled before the real practices for achieving immortality can fully take effect. Once they do, a man can live off the essence of things alone: dew, or ethereal emanations from the cosmos. The technique called the Five Germs enables him to absorb the "breaths" of the Five Elements to strengthen the Five Viscera. Or he may prefer to absorb the emanations of the sun. All these ways of feeding on emanations or breaths are refinements of ancient breathing methods whose main rule was: "Spit out the old [breath], and bring in the new [breath]," breathing in through the nose and out through the mouth. But the world itself breathes, so that the air is either alive (fresh) or dead (stale). The air is alive between midnight and noon, and dead between noon and midnight. Consequently, the breathing exercises have to be done during the time the air is alive. Instead of breathing normally, the adept aims at making the "breaths of the Nine Heavens, which came in through the nose, travel all around the body and flow into the Palace of the Brain." The breath is guided at the adept's will by the "inward vision." This is achieved by concentration and introspection (in the Chinese sense: the interior gaze that sees but also illumines), and results in a visualization of the breaths, sometimes in the form of a homunculus. The breath can thus be led to a sick part of the body, where it removes the obstruction causing the illness. One particular technique, called embryonic respiration, consists of making an internal "breath" go around the body in lieu of air actually breathed in; this method is practically the same as the internal alchemy discussed below.

The breathing techniques are generally supplemented by gymnastic, sexual, and dietary observances. Gymnastics makes it easier for the breath to circulate by loosening up the body and eliminating obstacles in the internal ducts. The aim behind the sexual practices, which go back as far as Han days, is to avoid the expenditure of vital energy involved in "the union of the Yin and the Yang." Normally, they are performed by two Taoist partners, in which case both benefit from it. But some Taoists use uninitiated women to increase their own vitality at their partner's expense; this kind of vampirism is condemned as unorthodox.

However, all these methods have only secondary importance for the schools that are primarily concerned with seeking medicines and foodstuffs capable of prolonging life or even of giving physical immortality. This is why the *Pen Ts'ao* (Great Pharmacopoeia) is included in the *Tao Tsang*. Its first author was none other than Shen Nung, the Divine Plowman, one of the first mythical rulers, who was the first to collect herbs and sample their effects. Yet the *Pen Ts'ao* is not concerned merely with medicinal plants; it also lists minerals and animal products. Not all these drugs had the same interest from the Taoist point of view. The *Pao P'u Tzu* distinguishes between three categories of drugs according to their effects: the higher ones give immortality; those of the second category prolong life; those of the third category, comprising mainly herbs, cure sickness.

Among the higher drugs we find, in order of decreasing importance: cinnabar, gold, silver, the five mushrooms (and like substances), jade, mica, pearls, and orpiment. The herbs and precious minerals had to be collected in conformity with complicated timetables (the moment was not always propitious), secret formulas, and magic signs. For instance, Ko Hung attaches great importance to talismans and other indispensable techniques for protecting oneself against evil influences or for winning the support of the spirits.

Tradition has it that the magic talismans called *fu* were invented by Chang Tao-ling, the first Heavenly Master. It is interesting to note that this term *fu*, taken in its proper meaning, designated badges of office or contracts written down on small rectangles of bamboo or metal (or on sheets of paper) and then cut into two, each party to the contract keeping one of the tallies thus formed. It seems that the *fu* of the Heavenly Masters, which were healing charms, guaranteed a sort of contract made with the gods; for the adepts of this sect, in accordance with a revelation made by Lao Tzu to Chang Tao-ling, swore not to sin in return for the assurance that they would never fall ill. But talismans were in use in almost all the sects, and were an important element in all the ceremonies. A *tao-shih* (master Taoist) intending to go into the mountains in search of long-life drugs would never leave without his magic charms. Ko Hung is quite explicit on this point: without a talisman, not only do you risk falling victim to the myriad spirits that haunt these desert spots, but also the mountain fairies hide the drugs so that you cannot find them. The same author mentions certain talismans that went in groups of fives because they acted either on the five space-time sectors of the cosmos or on each of the Five Sacred Peaks, which had the function of attracting all the sacred powers in their territory. Nowadays, the talismans distributed by the *tao-shih* have mainly medical or psychotherapeutic uses: easing childbirth, curing certain aches and pains, and calming sick people or frightened children.

The Taoists also offer other means of confronting the supernatural powers: perhaps the most remarkable are the magic dances. The most famous is the Yü dance, which goes back to very ancient times. Yü the Great, while laboring to stop the great flood, worked so hard that he ended up limping; his walk is supposed to be the origin behind his "step." But others say that heavenly spirits taught Yü this dance to give him command over the spirits of nature; still others claim that it is copied from the dance of strange birds, which use it to break up stones. It is a hopping dance that the sorcerers often perform in a state of trance. But the *tao-shih* consider its effectiveness to lie above all in the line traced by the officiant's feet, a line that reproduces the meander of the Great Bear or other labyrinthine shapes. As described by Ko Hung in a chapter devoted to "methods for climbing mountains and fording rivers," this dance step had the same effectiveness as the talismans.

THE ALCHEMISTS

As we have seen, Ko Hung considered the best long-life drugs to be cinnabar and gold. It was the alchemists' business to try to produce these substances. The first textual reference to alchemy is in the second century B.C., but it had certainly existed as an adjunct to metalworking and kindred arts long before that. When Emperor Wu was thinking of celebrating solemn sacrifices on T'ai Shan, the Sacred Peak of the East, the magicians living at his court cited the example of Huang Ti, who cast a sacred metal crucible before ascending in triumph to heaven. One of these magicians was admitted to the emperor's presence "because he was acquainted with the art of sacrificing to the furnace, and the methods for abstaining from cereals and for never growing old." He told the emperor: "Sacrifice to the furnace, and you can call forth the supernatural creatures. Then cinnabar powder can be changed to gold; when the gold has been produced, if you have drinking and eating utensils made from it, you will increase your longevity. Then you will be able to see the Blessed Immortals of P'eng-lai Island, in the middle of the sea. When you have seen them and made the Feng and Shan sacrifices, you will never die: that is what happened to Huang Ti."* After hearing these words, Emperor Wu made the sacrifice to the furnace for the first time, then busied himself with transmuting cinnabar powder and other drugs in order to obtain gold.

The furnace in question is, of course, the alchemical furnace; the sacrifice made to it was intended to attract spirits that would favor the formation of magic gold; by eating from dishes made of the gold, the emperor would increase his vital energy—his "holiness"—sufficiently to enter into relations with the Immortals and, after celebrating the solemn sacrifices to Heaven and Earth, become a *hsien-jen* himself.

Gold and cinnabar were always the two main ingredients in Chinese alchemy, the first because of its incorruptibility, the second because of its color and chemical properties. For many years the cinnabar used was that occurring naturally in several provinces. But from the Han period onward it was obtained artificially by the reaction of sulphur and saltpeter with mercury: this fine red cinnabar is used for the manufacture of vermilion. From Han times on, the alchemists also attempted to produce artificial gold. Some thought success lay in the amalgamation of mercury with other substances. When alchemy had become a specifically Taoist science, its aim was no longer the fabrication of magic plates and dishes, as it had been under Emperor Wu, but the preparation of the elixir of immortality by the transmutation of chemical substances.

The earliest alchemical treatise is the work of Wei Po-

* Ssu-ma Ch'ien, *Shih Chi*, Chap. 28, "The Feng and Shan Sacrifices," in the translation by Edouard Chavannes, *Les Mémoires historiques de Se-ma Ts'ien* (Paris, 1895–1905), III, 465. See also Burton Watson, trans., *Records of the Grand Historian of China* (New York and London, 1961), II, 39.

yang, who is believed to have written toward the middle of the second century A.D. It is called *Chou-i Ts'an T'ung Ch'i,* the exact meaning of which is uncertain: *Kinship of the Three Ways of Heaven, Earth, and Man,* or *Kinship of the Three Ways of the I Ching, Taoism, and Alchemy.* Essentially, the work deals with the production of the cinnabar used for the pill of immortality; but it uses an esoteric terminology that is incomprehensible to the uninitiated. Nonetheless, the text has been glossed on several occasions; although the interpretations differ on certain points, these commentaries do make the text less recondite. The central idea is that natural mutations can be speeded up in the alchemical crucible. In particular, it is possible to obtain purified cinnabar by subjecting it to a series of sublimations. When absorbed by the body, this cinnabar "dissipates the harmful vapors in the body and fumigates the four members to their extremities, whereupon the complexion becomes wonderfully clear, white hairs turn black, and teeth grow again where they had fallen out; old men grow young again, and from old women one gets young girls. It is possible to change one's appearance in order to escape from worldly peril. Such men deserve the name *chen-jen* [a Pure Man, i.e. a Holy Man who has regained his original pure nature]."

It was generally admitted that man's essential life principle was composed of "Primordial Breath" (*yüan-ch'i*), in other words a fragment of chaos, though some authors held that this essence was a mixture of Yin and Yang, the differentiations that occurred within chaos when the universe took form. Sickness and death are caused by an imbalance of Yin and Yang within the body, resulting in the loss of some of this breath. Physicians can increase this breath when it is deficient, but, according to the alchemists, only cinnabar and gold can really restore to the human body the primordial state in which the Yin and the Yang were so closely united that they could not be distinguished from each other. This was the meaning they gave to Lao Tzu's injunction "Embrace the Unity."

After Wei Po-yang, the greatest theoretician of alchemy was Ko Hung, the author of the *Pao P'u Tzu*. In point of fact, Ko Hung admits that he never undertook any experiments, because they were very expensive and he was poor. But he inherited a large library from his master; the list that he gives of it comprises the earliest catalog of Taoist writings to have come down to us. Among these books, the alchemical writings were particularly occult.

Pao P'u Tzu admits the usefulness of non-alchemical medicines, but affirms that they do not confer immortality, and he cites a saying of Lao Tzu's: "If you do not get the sublimated cinnabar and the liquor of gold, you will give yourself a lot of bother for nothing." Ko Hung explains the marvelous properties of gold and cinnabar as follows:

> Cinnabar, the more it is heated, the more admirable its changes are. Gold, put in the flames and melted a hundred times, will not change; buried, it will not become tainted, even to the end of time. If these two substances are eaten, they bring about a sublimation in the human body. . . .
> The least effective property of cinnabar is far superior to the best species of medicinal plants. When plants are burned, they turn to ashes, whereas grains of cinnabar, when heated, produce quicksilver; if the sublimation is continued, cinnabar is obtained anew.
>
> [Chapter 4]

Ko Hung gives a series of formulas taken from several different works, but the supreme method, the one enabling a man to ascend to heaven at the height of the day, is that called the Ninefold Transmutation. At each transmutation or sublimation, the cinnabar obtained is slightly more effective:

For immortality, take cinnabar of the first transmutation for three years; with cinnabar of the second transmutation, take it for two years, . . . and when you get to cinnabar of the ninth transmutation, simply take it for three consecutive days. . . . Pao P'u Tzu says: "Ninefold-transmuted cinnabar is indeed the best of all drugs for immortality, but it requires many ingredients that are hard to get, especially in times of unrest. Further, the fire has to be carefully watched so that its intensity is properly adjusted to the different phases in the operation." [Chapter 4]

Ko Hung says all this is extremely taxing and hard to achieve.

Despite his assertion that he himself had never experimented, Pao P'u Tzu seems to have been more interested in alchemical experimentation than Wei Po-yang ever was; on the other hand, the latter appears to have been the first of the theoreticians. For there were two traditions: the laboratory tradition and the theoretical tradition. This does not mean to say that there were no links between the two; but the second, which expressed itself more esoterically, led to new departures in alchemical theory, and to the emergence of what was called "internal cinnabar" (*nei tan*) as opposed to practical alchemy, called "external cinnabar" (*wai tan*).

NEI TAN

This theoretical internal alchemy contests the belief held by alchemists that gross substances such as mercury, cinnabar, earth, or metals can transform the human organism and make men immortal. Wei Po-yang's terminology must be taken to mean, not chemical substances, but cosmic influences working on two levels: in the macrocosm and in the microcosm.

These influences are symbolized by the trigrams and hexagrams (*kua*) found in the *I Ching*: first come the two basic *kua*, Heaven and Earth (*ch'ien* and *k'un*), the first formed of purely Yang lines and the second of purely Yin lines, which the *Ts'an T'ung Ch'i* calls the Gates to the Changes (i.e. their starting point) and the Father and Mother of all the other *kua*; then come the *kua* called *k'an* and *li*, which have the peculiarity—common to them and *ch'ien* and *k'un*—of not changing if they are turned upside down. *K'an* and *li* are the activity of *ch'ien* and *k'un*, i.e. the influences of Heaven and Earth. In alchemical terms, *ch'ien* and *k'un* are the furnace and the crucible; *k'an* and *li* are the ingredients combining to form the elixir. Hence these four *kua* are the fundamental symbols; the 60 remaining hexagrams represent the timing of the operation.

In internal alchemy, the human body is considered to be a tripod endowed by Heaven and Earth with the two life-constituents Yin and Yang; but this vital Yin contains some Yang and the Yang contains some Yin, so they are symbolized by *k'an* and *li*. These two trigrams represent the sacred union of *ch'ien* and *k'un* and, in a general way, that of the Yin and the Yang. The union is also said to be a union of the solar and lunar principles, for in the *I Ching*, *k'an* and *li* represent the moon and the sun. Mythology has it that a crow (Yin) dwells in the sun and a rabbit (Yang) lives in the moon, where he grinds up the ingredients of the elixir of immortality.

The alchemist's crucible and the human body are microcosms: the first is said to be like an egg composed of two halves (Heaven and Earth). When the halves fit closely together, they represent primordial chaos. In the same way, the head is *ch'ien* and the belly is *k'un*: these two "breaths" go up and down just like the emanations of Heaven and Earth, the union of which gives birth to all creatures. In the body, this circulation acts via two blood vessels, one for the Yin (the *jen* vein), another for the Yang (the *tu* vein), which are the two main lines of communication between the upper and lower parts of the body. Here the commentators frequently refer to Chapter 6 of the *Lao Tzu* (the Valley Spirit), which is supposed to be a veiled reference to these internal circulations and sacred unions. Allusions to the *Tao Te Ching* are plentiful in the *Ts'an T'ung Ch'i*, which interprets certain apothegms in an alchemical sense. Because this work also contains a lot of sexual imagery, some Taoists took the imagery literally and thought the work was about so-called bedroom techniques (*fang-chung*). This interpretation is repudiated by most of the commentators, who, in the event, are certainly right.

Nei tan is thus a variant of embryonic respiration, a variant in which the processes are described in an esoteric terminology borrowed from alchemy. When practicing embryonic respiration, the adept returned, so to speak, to the state of the infant in its mother's womb. The circulation of the breath—which, as has been pointed out, was a fragment of *yüan-ch'i*, undifferentiated ether—took place in a closed circuit. It was fetched from the Sea of the Breath (*ch'i-hai*) near the Lower Field of Cinnabar where it was concentrated, and made to climb to the brain and then circulate through the body while normal breathing was reduced to a minimum.

In classical *nei tan*, however, the mergings and sublimations were brought about by relaxed concentration. The aim was to invert the vital processes that normally end in death. The *p'o* soul, the dark soul of passion that becomes an infernal spirit after death, preponderates in most men over *hun*, the soul of light. The result is that men indulge in passionate activities and waste their vital energies by externalizing them, above all during sexual activity. New creatures are then born, but the individual soon dies; his Yin and Yang principles disjoin and return to their separate origins, and the self disappears. The methods of *nei tan* make it possible to escape this "descent" of organic life and to bring about a resurgence of the life forces and a marriage of the Yin and Yang principles. Just as a woman must be submissive toward a man, *p'o* must be submissive toward *hun*—to their mutual profit. Instead of being externalized, the life forces must be concentrated inwardly and be independent of the perceptible world and its attractions. Instead of producing new creatures externally, the adept has to give birth to a new man within himself. This idea is symbolized by the alchemical image of the golden Pill of Life that rises sparkling from the crucible, or by that of a homunculus taking shape in the depths of the body, the offspring of the union of *k'an* and *li*. This infant represents the immortal soul that the Taoist strives to create; finally externalized at the moment when the great work is completed, the soul leaves the mortal body and ascends into heaven. The immortal soul thus produced by internal alchemy is also called the Golden Flower, which blossoms out once the individual has freed himself of all external attachments.*

MEDITATION

Embryonic respiration and *nei tan* are essentially mental operations, since it is thought processes that make the breath circulate through the body and that manipulate the internal alchemical symbols. One particular technique of concentration makes it possible to "gaze inward." While the breath circulates through the body, the eyes fix on it and follow its movement. Since the pupils of the eyes— small concretions of pure Yang—have an illumining power, they put darkness to flight and cause the triumph of the Yang, the principle of light and life.†

Internal vision also makes it possible to perceive various spirits or divinities that inhabit the body. The eyes, the ears, the hair and each of the viscera and other organs possess at least one of them. A number of treatises describe them precisely, give their names, and often provide a picture of them to make visualizing them and entering into communication with them easier. Since the body is a microcosm, all these interior divinities are also the gods of the exterior world. But this pantheon is so vast and complicated that to give a brief

* See *The Secret of the Golden Flower*, a *nei tan* treatise translated by Richard Wilhelm, with a preface by C. G. Jung. The book is illustrated with mandalas drawn, independently of any oriental influence, by European mental patients. Jung detected in them a parallel between the philosophy of the Far East and the European unconscious.

† A novel conception of the role played by the Yin and the Yang. In ancient and classical theory, they were held to collaborate; but this collaboration implies the alternation of life and death. The desire for eternal life naturally leads, therefore, to a desire for the victory of Yang over Yin.

account of it here is impossible. The role of all these gods, who were generally much of a piece, was above all to serve as aids to meditation, hooks to hang one's thoughts on. Certain early Taoists thought it was necessary to go out in search of the gods and Immortals in the solitude of the mountains. But the idea that it was sufficient to discover them in oneself rapidly supplanted this earlier belief. Chou I-shan, a legendary Taoist from the close of the Han, spent many years scouring the mountains and caves for the gods. He finally came across them:

> Then he closed his eyes in order to gaze inward; after a long wait, he indeed saw that inside the Eastern Chamber [one of the compartments of the head] there were two great gods [of the Triad], whose appearance and costumes were exactly as they had been on Mount K'ung [in the cave on the mountain].
> Lord Yellow Elder burst out laughing and said: Subtle! Profound! Use meditation—that is the way to ascend into heaven at the height of day.*

Meditation was called "concentrating on the One" or "keeping the One." In the days of Emperor Wu of the Han, the magicians instituted a cult of the Supreme One (T'ai I), then the Three Ones (the One of Heaven, the One of Earth, and the T'ai I). In later Taoism, each of these three divinities was imagined to dwell in one of the three Fields of Cinnabar. In point of fact, this unity remained a single whole, although it was mentally "visualized" in three dwelling places.

The earliest description of meditation on the One is

---

* Tzu-yang chen-jen nei-chuan," in *Tao Tsung* (Taoist Canon) (Shanghai, 1924–26), fascicle 152, quoted in Henri Maspero, "Le Taoïsme," Vol. 2 of *Mélanges posthumes sur les religions et l'histoire de la Chine* (Paris, 1950), p. 138.

found in the *T'ai P'ing Ching* under the title *Shou I Ming Fa* (How to Concentrate on the Light of the One):

The method for keeping the light of the One is the basis of the art of long life. It enables a man to seek the divinities and to get them to come out of the abode of brilliant light. Keeping the light of the One is this: as soon as the first small tongue of flame is perceived, its image must be retained and not lost for a second. At first, it is entirely red; then it turns white, and eventually entirely green. It is a brightness that seems to spread farther and farther. But it has to be brought back and unified; inside, everything will be illumined. This eliminates all sickness; if it [the inward light] is kept unfailingly, this process can be said to be the art of living for ten thousand years.

This visualization of the light during meditation was certainly practiced from a very early date. As we have seen, Lao Tzu often mentions an interior light. Huai-nan Tzu, repeating a saying of Chuang Tzu's, compares the Holy Man's heart (i.e. his mind) to an empty room in which a light appears, the sign of the presence of the Tao. Later, the method for keeping the One involved not only light visions, but also the apparition of the divinities (the Three Ones), which were said to come into being by transformation within the adept.

Comparable methods of meditation accompanied all the religious observances. Thus, before reciting the *Ling Pao Tu Jen Ching* (The Marvelous Talisman Book of the Salvation of Men), a revealed book that for many years was one of the most important texts in Taoism, the adept, after observing the preliminary abstinences and performing the purificatory ablutions, had to proceed as follows: half closing his eyes, he offered a mental greeting to the sovereigns of the 32 heavens, starting with the east; then, closing his eyes completely, he imagined three vapors—green, yellow, and white—rising up from beneath his seat and soon filling the whole room. On his left was the Green Dragon, on his right the White Tiger, in front of him the Red Bird, behind him the Dark Warrior. In addition, on his right and left, he saw two rows of eight lions and two rows of eight white cranes. Further, the room was illumined by the Sun in front of him, and the Moon behind him. From the nape of his neck emanated an aureole of light rays that illumined the ten spatial directions. All this had to be perceived with great clarity. The adept then pronounced a prayer addressed to Tao Chün to inform him of the purpose of the recitation.

By means of this preliminary meditation, the Taoist extracts the cosmic emblems from within himself and projects them around himself to form a mental mandala—an image of the world at whose center he himself appears deified, the necessary condition for entering into communication with the gods. In the sects that practiced liturgical recitation of the *Tao Te Ching*, the recitation was preceded by a meditation comparable to the one we have just described. Sometimes the mandala is reduced to a mere circle representing the Void of the Tao—a representation that has certain affinities with the spirit of philosophical Taoism. This is how the adepts of Zen sometimes represent Bodhidharma, the founder of the sect: a silhouette within a circle.

THE SACRED TEXTS AND THE REVELATIONS

The ancient Chinese believed that Heaven (or the Heavenly Ruler, T'ien Ti) reacted to the conduct of the earthly monarch: warnings in the form of ill omens, if unheeded, led to calamities, but virtue was acknowledged by favorable signs in nature or, better still, by the miraculous appearance of auspicious creatures or objects. These objects were preserved in the royal treasury and had sacred value as symbols of the "Heavenly Mandate." Some of them were dynastic talismans; others were texts, the most famous of which were the *Ho T'u* (Chart of the Yellow River) and the *Lo Shu* (Book of Lo River). These and similar signs from Heaven were carefully recorded by the Han historians and their successors.

The *T'ai P'ing Ching*, the most important sacred book in religious Taoism after the *Tao Te Ching*, first appeared at a time when the virtue of the Han seemed to be declining; it was twice presented at court as a scripture mysteriously discovered at the side of a river, which reminds us of the prototypes, *Ho T'u* and *Lo Shu*. This text, it was said, could bring new prosperity to the dynasty and renew its apparently diminishing fecundity. This revelation benefited, not the Han emperors, but the religious leaders of the Yellow Turbans and, later, the Heavenly Masters of the Five Bushel Sect. The text preserved in the Taoist collection, though incomplete and recompiled in the seventh century, has certainly kept the main ideas of the original. Apart from an account of the moral and political utopia T'ai P'ing, it contains many teachings typical of later Taoism. These teachings, which have to do with meditation and "cultivating the life principle," belong to the corpus of rules that the monarch must follow in order to bring about a new Golden Age; this idea lingered on in the other sects. Besides the various passages on concentration, one of which has been quoted earlier, this book contains teachings on hygiene, respiration, and diet; they generally amount to saying "get in harmony with nature." Mention is made of magic formulas and medicinal talismans (*fu*) that were taken as cures. The plants that give immortality are said to exist in Heaven, where they belong to a hierarchy, their efficacy depending on their rank in this hierarchy; they come down to earth only for virtuous people. Sick people are sinners and, theoretically, the only cure for them is repentance; but in practice they were also given treatments of moxa* and acupuncture. The point is also made that people can be sick because of a sin of some ancestor as well as for sins of their own, because sin is hereditary.

During the Chinese Middle Ages, the *T'ai P'ing Ching* was superseded by other sacred books. These were the texts around which the three main sections (the three *tung*) of the *Tao Tsang* came to be formed. The *Shang Ch'ing Ching* (Book of the Heaven of Superior Purity), or *Ta Tung Chen Ching*, the basic text of the Tung Chen section, was revealed to a medium. Members of the important Mao Shan sect established on Mount Mao near modern Nanking conducted experiments in automatic writing, during which texts were dictated to mediums by Taoist Immortals. This sūtra is essentially a sort of liturgical poem in four- or five-stress lines; reciting the sūtra is considered efficacious because it contains the secret names of the spirits and gods invoked. These spirits were believed to dwell simultaneously in Heaven, in the sacred mountains, and above all in the microcosm of the adept's own body: there is a close connection between these three domains, and the practices of Taoism aim essentially at preserving or reestablish-

---

* Moxa is a soft woolly mass prepared from the young leaves of various eastern Asia wormwoods and used as a cautery by being ignited on the skin. The term is sometimes extended to include other substances used in the same manner.

ing this connection. It is worth pointing out that, in this sect, female Immortals play an important role: they are the mediators without whom no revelations can occur. Moreover, the first leader of the Mao Shan was a woman, Lady Wei: she had the revelation of a book that plays an essential role in the practices relating to "nurture of the life principle," the *Huang T'ing Ching* (Book of the Yellow Court). It is an essential work because it discusses the interior gods and reveals their names. The *Shang Ch'ing Ching* is concerned with the liturgical application of the highly cryptic teachings of the *Huang T'ing Ching*.

Another important book, which appeared in the same circles, though at an earlier date, is the *San Huang Ching* (Book of the Three Great Men). This text was revealed to a Taoist while he was contemplating the wall of a cave. Originally, it seems, the text consisted of a series of talismans (*fu*); the ancillary texts, dealing mainly with magical practices (e.g. how to fight demons), were added later.

Two other books, texts in which the Tung Hsüan section of the *Tao Tsang* originated, both go by the name *Ling Pao Ching* (Book of the Marvelous Jewel, or better, Book of the Marvelous Talisman). The earlier *Ling Pao Ching* was a series of five talismans, hence its title *Ling Pao Wu Fu Ching* (Book of the Five Ling Pao Talismans); it had other texts added to it at a later date, probably in the third or early fourth century. Later still, in the second half of the fourth century, another *Ling Pao Ching* was substituted for the first, clearly with the intention of combating the influence of Mahayanist Buddhism. The title of this later work is *Ling Pao Tu Jen Ching* (The Marvelous Talisman Book of the Salvation of Men). It gives a portrait of Yüan Shih T'ien Tsun modeled on the portraits of the compassionate

Buddhas and Bodhisattvas. At the beginning of a Kalpa,* Yüan Shih T'ien Tsun, the supreme divinity, recited the sacred text for the first time. (The characters of the text are said to be an emanation of primordial chaos, a crystallization of the original Breath.) This first recitation took place inside a pearl (symbol of the Tao), which the god and his disciples miraculously entered while the heavens stopped revolving and the earth became flat. Taoists who recite this book ten times over, as Yüan Shih T'ien Tsun did, invoke the gods of the ten directions of the universe and, by their prayers, ask them to cure all kinds of evils; above all, they can obtain by this means the deliverance of the souls of the dead imprisoned in the underworld and cause them to be reborn in the regions of Heaven. This text has a strong Buddhist flavor: the concern is not only with one's own salvation, but also with the salvation of others. Nevertheless, the spirit of Taoism is not altogether absent: for one thing, the gods are inside the microcosm, and for another, prayer is efficacious solely because this microcosm is reconstituted as a whole by the liturgy—which amounts to saying that, between the interior and the exterior, between the microcosm and the macrocosm, there is no longer any distinction.

* Kalpa is a Buddhist term for a cosmic cycle extending from the creation to the destruction of a world system.

CONCLUSION

Taoism as a whole is a complex and often disconcerting phenomenon: side by side, we find profound insight and puerile suppositions, lofty mysticism and superstitious magic, exhortations to absolute purity and the most primitive obscenity. It must be said at once that these contradictions are often only apparent: Taoist minds and Western minds (perhaps we should say modern minds) categorize their thoughts quite differently. Yet the synthetic, "organicist" thinking of the ancient Chinese is proving worthier of interest as our knowledge of it increases. This is as true for the history of science as for the history of ideas: the very mysticism of the fathers of Taoism contained some elements that could have favored the rise of a scientific movement. Other factors prevented this from happening, but the Taoist spirit contributed largely to the growth of the graphic arts and many crafts.*

The fact remains that, because of the anarchical way it developed, Taoism is very heteroclite. From the very earliest days, the philosophers were exposed to all kinds of influences: literati, hermits, artisans, magicians, and priests and priestesses of the popular religion. Even in later peri-

* See Joseph Needham, *Science and Civilisation in China* (Cambridge, Eng., 1956), II, 33f.

ods, religious Taoism was never brought under the discipline of a central spiritual authority; the doctrine was never organized into a system or expressed in a dogma. This accounts for the proliferation of sects, some esoteric, others open to all. The Taoists replied to the challenge of Buddhism by borrowing some of its ideas (retribution and reincarnation) and institutions (monasticism). But, like everything else in Taoism, the Buddhist-inspired Taoist hell is unmistakably Chinese.

One of the most interesting aspects of Taoism is *nei tan*. Whereas the Confucians hold that a man's whole life depends on Destiny (*ming*: decree of Heaven), the Taoist adepts of *nei tan* believe that our destiny depends on ourselves and not on Heaven. True, these introverts seem to limit the application of this precept to their own internal hygiene, but we should remember that increasing one's vital potency (Te) is a prerequisite, if not for acting, at least for influencing others. As we have seen, the *nei tan* exercises go together with the elimination from consciousness of everything extraneous to pure self, which means expelling the social self in favor of a cosmic self—a unified, global, and potent consciousness instead of a plethora of lesser states of awareness. Even the most bizarre *nei tan* techniques aim at achieving this higher state of consciousness, which is held to confer, not immortality, in which few educated people still believe, but prolonged youth.

It seems that Taoism can no longer be practiced openly in continental China, but in Taiwan it still has a remarkable following. Its close links with popular religion have led some observers to confuse the two. In fact, very large numbers of Taoist temples exist on the island, some of them old, very many others brand new. The *tao-shih*, who belong to the Heavenly Masters Sect, still observe the same age-old liturgy. This continuity is remarkable, when we think that the tradition was established by the first Heavenly Masters nearly two thousand years ago. The funeral ritual is very impressive. The *tao-shih* also officiate for village or urban communities on the occasion of important periodic festivals. It is these occasions that have given rise to the confusion mentioned above: the strictly Taoist ceremony takes place inside the temple while the popular celebrations go on simultaneously outside, a kind of carnival entailing ostentatious display and squandering of the community's wealth. But let there be no mistake about this: for Taoists, the serious business happens inside, where the gods come to dwell within the main officiant, who convokes them by his prayers and contemplates them with his "inner gaze."

In addition to this Taoism with popular affinities, a more official Taoism is gaining ground on the island thanks to the initiative of Chang En-p'u, the latest in the line of Heavenly Masters, who has claimed sanctuary at Taipei.* Chang En-p'u is said to be the sixty-third member of the same Chang family to hold the rank of Heavenly Master in the succession that began with Chang Tao-ling. The Heavenly Masters lead the Cheng-i sect, which, together with the Ch'üan-chen sect, is the most representative of all the modern Taoist sects since the Sung dynasty. The Cheng-i specializes in magical practices. Chang En-p'u still prepares talismans, confers diplomas on priests, and conducts ceremonies at festivals or upon private request. Be-

---

* See Holmes Welch, "The Shang T'ien Shih and Taoism in China," *Journal of Oriental Studies*, Vol. IV, Nos. 1–2 (1957–58).

sides this, he has set up two associations, the Adepts of Taoism (about a hundred members in 1958) and the Taiwan Taoist Association (four thousand members in 1958).

The Ch'üan-chen sect, more recent than the Cheng-i, is also known as the Internal Alchemy Sect, Tan-ting. The famous White Clouds Monastery (Po Yün Kuan) in Peking was one of its dependencies. Whereas Cheng-i priests are married, Ch'üan-chen monks practice celibacy; there seems to be no Ch'üan-chen monastery on Taiwan, but there are 2,800 Taoist temples. The lay adepts of Ch'üan-chen have no form of collective observance, but perform daily meditation and charitable works.

If we ask what future there can be for Taoism, the answer, at first flush, must be rather pessimistic. On the continent, the Communists are particularly hostile toward Taoism because it is suspected of housing subversive secret societies. Even in Taiwan, Taoism has a poor reputation among officials and intellectuals. Some of them realize, however, that this religion, which has counted for so much in traditional Chinese culture, merits respect: it is, after all, the only truly national religion; for Confucianism is not, strictly speaking, a religion, and Buddhism came in from abroad. On the other hand, Taoism's connection with popular beliefs and practices, some of which are wrongly held to be superstitions, does it much harm. And then, Chinese scholars who readily parse the thought and language of the *Lao Tzu* or the *Chuang Tzu* generally know little about popular customs, village Taoism included, even though the aboriginal inhabitants of the island, like the mountain peoples of South China before them, have been the object of thorough ethnological surveys. This state of affairs is unfortunate, for there is every reason to believe that religious Taoism is destined to disappear, in its present form at least, if only to adapt itself to modern conditions.

Philosophical Taoism still arouses considerable interest throughout the world, as can be seen from the innumerable translations of the *Tao Te Ching* published in the West and the many studies of it published in China and Japan. One reason for the extraordinary appeal of this short text is certainly the cryptic nature of the apothegms themselves; another, perhaps, is that our frantic world is fond of hearing about the virtues of *wu-wei* and absolute tranquillity. In a sense, the doctrine of nonintervention accords perfectly with our conception of the true scientific spirit, which, first and foremost, means respect for natural laws. But by way of antithesis, the real interest of Taoism for us today lies in the psychological value of some aspects of it (very close to Yoga) and, above all, in its spiritual content.

Bibliography and Index

SELECTED BIBLIOGRAPHY

PRIMARY SOURCES

Chuang Tzu. *Chuang Tzu: Basic Writings*. Burton Watson, trans. New York and London, 1964.

———. *Chuang Tzu: Taoist Philosopher and Chinese Mystic*. Herbert A. Giles, trans. 2d ed. rev., reprinted. London, 1961.

Ko Hung. *Pao P'u Tzu*. Eugène Feifel, trans., in *Monumenta Serica*, VI (1941), 113–211; IX (1944), 1–33; and XI (1946), 1–32.

———. *Alchemy, Medicine, Religion in the China of* A.D. *320: The Nei P'ien of Ko Hung (Pao P'u Tzu)*. James R. Ware, trans. Cambridge, Mass., 1966.

———. *Tao Te Ching: The Book of the Way and Its Virtue*. J. J. L. Duyvendak, trans. London, 1954.

———. *The Way of Lao Tzu*. Wing-tsit Chan, trans. Indianapolis, 1963.

———. *The Way and Its Power*. Arthur Waley, trans. London, 1934.

Le Lie-sien tchouan: Biographies légendaires. Max Kaltenmark, trans. Peking, 1953.

Les Pères du système taoïste. Léon Wieger, trans. Sienhsien, 1913.

The Secret of the Golden Flower. Richard Wilhelm, trans. London, 1931.

A Source Book in Chinese Philosophy. Wing-tsit Chan, trans. and comp. Princeton, N.J., 1963.

Ssu-ma Ch'ien. *Les Mémoires historiques de Se-ma Ts'ien*. Edouard Chavannes, trans. 5 vols. Paris, 1895–1905.

———. *Records of the Grand Historian of China*. Burton Watson, trans. 2 vols. New York and London, 1961.

The Texts of Taoism. James Legge, trans. London, 1881.

Chavannes, Edouard. "Le Jet des Dragons," in *Mémoires concernant l'Asie orientale*, Vol. 3. Paris, 1919.

SECONDARY SOURCES

Demiéville, Paul. "La Situation religieuse en Chine au temps de Marco Polo," in *Oriente Poliana*, pp. 193–234. Rome, 1957.

Dore, Henri. "Lao tseu et le Taoïsme," in *Recherches sur les superstitions en Chine*, Vol. 18, Part 3, Section 3.

Eichhorn, Werner. "Bemerkungen zum Aufstand des Chang Chio und zum Staate des Chang Lu," *Mitteilungen des Instituts für Orientforschung*, Vol. 3, No. 2 (1955), 325–52.

——. "T'ai-p'ing und T'ai-p'ing Religion," *Mitteilungen des Instituts für Orientforschung*, Vol. 5, No. 1 (1957).

Fung Yu-lan. *A History of Chinese Philosophy*. Derk Bodde, trans. 2 vols. Princeton, N.J., 1952–53.

Granet, Marcel. *La Pensée chinoise*. Paris, 1934.

——. "Remarques sur le Taoïsme ancien," *Asia Major*, Vol. 2, pp. 146–51. Reprinted in *Etudes sociologiques sur la Chine*. Paris, 1953.

Groot, J. J. M. de. *The Religious System of China*. 6 vols. Leiden, 1892–1910.

Kaltenmark, Max. "Ling-pao: Note sur un terme du Taoïsme religieux," in *Mélanges publiés par l'Institut des Hautes Etudes Chinoises*, Vol. 2. Paris, 1960.

Maspero, Henri. "Les Procédés de nourrir le principe vital dans la religion taoïste ancienne," *Journal Asiatique* (1937).

——. *Le Taoïsme*. Vol 2 of *Mélanges posthumes sur les religions et l'histoire de la Chine*. Paris, 1950.

Needham, Joseph. *Science and Civilisation in China*, Vol. 2. Cambridge, Eng., 1956.

Schipper, Kristopher. *L'Empereur Wou des Han dans la légende taoïste*. Paris, 1965.

Stein, R. A. "Remarques sur les mouvements du Taoïsme politico-religieux au IIe siècle ap. J.-C.," *T'oung-pao*, 50 (1963), 1–78.

Vandermeersch, Léon. *La Formation du Légisme*. Paris, 1965.

Welch, Holmes. *Taoism: The Parting of the Way*. Boston, 1966.

Wright, Arthur F., ed. *Studies in Chinese Thought*. Chicago, 1953.

INDEX